Learning to talk

Learning to talk

JOHN McSHANE
Lecturer in Psychology
University of St Andrews

CAMBRIDGE UNIVERSITY PRESS

CAMBRIDGE
LONDON   NEW YORK   NEW ROCHELLE
MELBOURNE   SYDNEY

Published by the Press Syndicate of the University of Cambridge
The Pitt Building, Trumpington Street, Cambridge CB2 1RP
32 East 57th Street, New York, NY 10022, USA
296 Beaconsfield Parade, Middle Park, Melbourne 3206, Australia

© Cambridge University Press 1980

First published 1980

Printed in Great Britain at the University Press, Cambridge

Library of Congress Cataloguing in Publication Data
McShane, John, 1949–
Learning to talk.
Bibliography: p.
Includes index.
1. Language acquisition. I. Title.
PI18.M326 1980   401'.9   79-19875
ISBN 0 521 22478 0

For Benjamin, Clare, Jessica, Jenny, Karen, and Tom

We shall not cease from exploration
And the end of all our exploring
Will be to arrive where we started
And know the place for the first time

T. S. Eliot, 'Little Gidding'

Contents

Contents

Contents

Acknowledgements

The research on which this book is based was carried out at Cambridge University and I am grateful for the facilities provided by the Psychological Laboratory. I had many helpful discussions with Brian Butterworth and Elena Lieven at Cambridge, and John Gray and Robert Hoogenraad at St Andrews. The reliability studies were carried out by Chris Henshall and Elena Lieven; their assistance is much appreciated. I am grateful to Jerome Bruner and Martin Richards for their encouragement to publish this work. Margaret Smith was an invaluable typist. Above all, I would like to thank the children and their parents without whose cooperation this study would not have been possible, and my wife, Phil, for her support and encouragement during all of this.

A note on notation

Much of what I have to say concerns speech. I have used italics to cite utterances and to refer to utterances. I have used single quotation marks to refer to words when the meaning of a word is being discussed. The complete index of notation is as follows:

Italics
1. For utterances.
2. For emphasis.
3. For book titles.
4. For symbols.
5. For foreign words and phrases.

Single quotation marks
1. For the expression contained therein.

Double quotation marks
1. For quotation from other authors.
2. For theoretical terms on occasion.
3. As scare quotes.
4. When providing a gloss for an utterance.

1

Identifying the issues

1.0 Words and utterances

The fundamental question to which this book addresses itself is a simple one: how do children learn to talk? A child at the age of 2 years is well on the way to learning a language. He or she will have a sizeable vocabulary and will speak utterances that exhibit grammatical structure (Brown, 1973). Contrast a child at the age of 1 year. Vocabulary, if it exists at all, will be limited to a few words and the child will certainly not speak any grammatically structured utterances. Between the ages of 1 and 2 most children will go through a period of several months when they will speak one word at a time. Their vocabularies will increase slowly at first, with only a few words being added per month, but quite often there will then be a rapid increase in vocabulary some time after the middle of the second year (Nelson, 1973). In the latter part of the second year children will begin to combine words together in a predictable and regular way to make structured utterances. And so we are back to the child at 2 years. What has been happening?

The initial answer that suggests itself is that children learn words and then learn to put words together to form sentences. There is an important element of truth in this answer but it is also seriously misleading. Words, *qua* words, do not have any salience for the child initially. "In the beginning was the word" is exactly wrong; in the beginning was the utterance. The argument that I wish to advance is that language development is best studied as the development of intentional vocal communication. This shifts the emphasis from words as structural units to utterances as functional communicative units and it gives a central place to the notion of utterer's meaning. Consider the following example.

Suppose a child was to utter the sound *mummy* to make a variety of requests from his or her mother, and suppose that the sound was never observed in use in any other context. An analysis of the utterer's meaning would state that *mummy* is used to request and the instances of the utterance would be instances of the speech-act of requesting. One might be tempted to ask the further question: what does the word 'mummy' mean; what concept does the word represent for the child? The answer might seem to be: the child's mother. This answer is not warranted by the evidence presented, since there are no more grounds for saying 'mummy' represents the child's mother than there would be for saying 'help' represents the child's mother if *help* were substituted for *mummy* in the initial description. The fact that 'mummy' would represent the child's mother in the adult lexicon (and that it will later come to do so in the lexicon of a child to whom the above description might apply) should not encourage the inference that it does so on the evidence presented above.

Suppose, on the other hand, that the same child at a later point in development was observed to utter *mummy*, when asked *who's that?* in some appropriate context; *mummy sock*, to make a statement about the ownership of a sock; *mummy look*, when directing the mother's attention. In these situations it seems obvious that 'mummy' is a linguistic element, a word, which can be combined with various other words to form different sorts of utterances. The argument that 'mummy' represents the child's mother now seems well founded.

What are the differences between the two cases? The most obvious difference is the nature of the evidence available. In evaluating this evidence I have placed emphasis on the child's behaviour and I have used the repertoire of behaviour to dictate the inferences that can be drawn about underlying processes. This is part of a general belief (which I shall not here defend) that we need to attribute to an organism cognitive structures sufficiently complex, but no more so, for the organization of the behaviours observed. In the initial example the child's behaviour is limited to one type of activity and there is no evidence that 'mummy' has a representational relationship with any concept. That particular inference is not warranted by the behavioural evidence. It should be noted that I am not claiming that the child lacks concepts; I am claiming that the evidence presented does not warrant the inference that 'mummy' conceptually represents the child's mother.

In the second example the child has advanced to the point where the word 'mummy' has the conceptual status of a name for the child's mother and the child's utterances also exhibit some minimum grammatical structure. Some explanation of that development is obviously necessary and I will attempt to provide it in Chapter 2. The main point here is that the meaning of a child's utterance does not relate in any necessary way to the meaning of the words uttered. I will call the two types of meaning 'utterer's meaning' and 'semantic meaning' respectively to preserve a clear distinction. Utterer's meaning is "what the speaker means by uttering X" and semantic meaning is "what X means". The former is the concern of participants and the latter is the concern of linguists (and participant pedants). There is no one-to-one connection between utterer's meaning and semantic meaning. Consider the utterance *it's time to finish*. Supply the appropriate context and it could be a statement, a warning, a threat, or a question. Utterer's meaning, being concerned with the specific utterance in its specific context, can capture these variations. Semantic meaning is less concerned with context, more with the permanent, decontextualized meaning of words and sentences. The remainder of this chapter is concerned with explicating the notion of utterer's meaning.

1.1 Utterer's meaning

The first detailed account of utterer's meaning was offered by Grice (1957). According to Grice a speaker S means something by an utterance if S intends to have a certain effect on an audience A by means of A's recognition of S's intention. Grice's account actually covers more than utterances, but discussion will be limited here to the case of utterances.

Two primary uses of language are those of making statements and issuing imperatives, and Grice (1957) attempted to analyse the conditions of meaning for these utterances by offering an account of what it is for someone to mean something by an utterance. The following account, in the Gricean spirit, derives from Bennett (1976) and from Schiffer (1972).

Statements:

If S utters X thereby meaning that P, S utters X intending

  (i)   that some audience A should come to have the activated belief that P^1,

 (ii) that A should be aware of intention (i), and

(iii) that the awareness mentioned in (ii) should be part of A's reason for having the activated belief that P.

Imperatives:

If S utters X thereby meaning that A is to do Y, S utters X intending

  (i)   that A should do Y,

 (ii) that A should be aware of intention (i), and

(iii) that the awareness mentioned in (ii) should be part of A's reason for doing Y.

This account of statements and imperatives is a general account of how a speaker can mean something by uttering. The burden of meaning is placed on the speaker's intentions and the audience's recognition of these intentions. How can intentions carry that burden?[2]

---

[1] As originally formulated Grice's theory claimed that in uttering a statement the speaker intends to get the audience to believe something. It may sometimes be the case, it may even generally be the case, that the speaker intends to get the audience to believe what it is told, but there will be cases where inducing belief is redundant, in that the audience may know, and the speaker may know that the audience knows, whatever fact it is that the speaker is drawing to the audience's attention. It seems odd to claim, in these cases, that the speaker intends to induce some belief in the audience. Grice (1968) has reformulated the conditions for statements by restating the intentional condition as: S intends A to think that S believes that P. This amendment removes the claim that the speaker always intends to induce belief in the audience. Unfortunately it also removes the claim that the speaker ever intends to do so, and Bennett (1976) has shown that the revision is inadequate. The formulation above was proposed by Schiffer (1972). The intentional condition for a statement is: S intends to give A the activated belief that P. This formulation covers cases where the speaker intends to get the audience to believe that P and cases where the speaker intends to remind the audience that P, to bring the belief that P to the front of the audience's mind, and so on.

[2] There are a number of objections to Grice's intentional conditions that I wish to place aside. These objections (Searle, 1969; Wilson, 1970; Ziff, 1967) aim to show that Grice's conditions are inadequate either in that there are clear cases of meaning that fall outside the scope of Grice's theory or in that there are clear cases of nonsense that fall within the scope of the theory. The most striking thing about these objections is their oddity and their remoteness from central cases of communication. Ziff objects that a man might utter meaningful statements while delirious and thereby utter meaningful statements

Searle (1969) has argued that the intentional bridge between speaker and audience is provided by the structure of their common language which provides a conventional means of conveying intentions. According to Searle (1969: 49–50) Grice's analysis of utterances should be replaced by the following:

If S utters X and means it (i.e. means literally what he or she says) S utters X intending

(i) that the utterance X produce in some audience A the knowledge (recognition, awareness) that the states of affairs specified by (certain of) the rules of X obtain (call this the illocutionary effect),

(ii) that X produce this effect by means of A's recognition of intention (i), and

(iii) that the recognition mentioned in (ii) occur in virtue of (by means of) A's knowledge of (certain of) the rules governing (the elements of) X.

Although Searle stresses the intentional component of the speaker's utterance his account locates the issue of expressing and understanding intentions within a network of established linguistic rules. No doubt adult language-users do understand each other in virtue, in part, of their mutual knowledge of the structure of language. But a model founded on this premise encounters a number of difficulties. Searle's account requires that the illocutionary force of an utterance be, in some sense, part of the meaning of the sentence uttered. While such an account works for some utterances it does not work for all. It deals plausibly only with literal utterances and beyond these cases Stampe (1975)

---

without having any Gricean intentions. Ziff's man is meaningful in virtue of the fact that his language is conventionally intelligible but *he* does not mean anything – he is raving. Wilson objects that he (Wilson) might utter (to Grice) *Snow is white* with the intention of reporting that snow is white but without the intention to induce belief; indeed with the specific intention not to have any intention that Grice might attribute to him. This leads to a paradox: Grice might see through Wilson's defence and respond *your intention is to avoid having any intention I attribute to you*. Will Wilson concede that that was his intention? Searle constructs the following scenario: An American soldier is captured by Italian troops during the Second World War. The American suspects that the Italians know very little German, so he utters the one German sentence he knows, intending to induce the Italians to believe that he is a German soldier so that they will release him. Searle's man is an incredible optimist. His intention is groundless.

At best these counterexamples are skirmishes on the periphery of cases of meaning. I am concerned with cases where speakers are in a condition to speak with intentions (unlike Ziff's man) and do not contrive to be at cross-purposes with their audience.

has documented the confusions inherent in any treatment of illocutionary force as a structural component of a sentence. But, even accepting that there is a partial truth in Searle's account, there is still an important epistemic issue unresolved for those cases where linguistic structure is a guide to the speaker's intentions: how do children learn to match intentions and linguistic structures? If children do not have an innate knowledge of linguistic structures how is meaning and understanding possible in the absence of such structures? Searle's account of utterer's meaning is of no help in such cases. The developmental route to utterer's meaning does not lie in Searle's formulation of how speakers express their intentions and expect to have these intentions understood. Grice's own theory is unaffected by all of this for Grice does not make any claim that the speaker has to utter structured sentences or that the audience relies on a knowledge of linguistic structure to interpret the speaker's utterances. Having thus deprived the development of meaning of a reliance on linguistic structure the next step must be to show how a communication system can exist in the absence of linguistic structure.

Bennett (1976) has provided a plausible account of how an intentional communication system might begin. To illustrate the point Bennett introduces a mythical tribe who do not yet have a structured language.

One day we observe a tribesman, U, stand in full view of another, A, and emit a snake-like hissing sound while also making with his hand a smooth, undulating, horizontal motion which resembles the movement of a snake. Why did he do this?   (1976: 138)

It is not difficult to construct the answer: U did it to warn A of a snake or snakes; nor is it difficult to see that U's warning might be effective. It is not a long step to:

U was relying on A's thinking that U intended to get A to believe that there was a snake nearby ('to believe P', for short); and he further expected that A would be led to believe P by his belief that U wanted him to believe P.   (1976: 140)

That makes the case of one meaning. On further occasions U and A might perform the same actions (possibly in opposite roles) to communicate the same message. They would have reason to do so if the first communication had been effective. Successive performances would establish a behavioural regularity. Gradually other tribesmen would learn the communication and in time it would pass into general use. Any tribesman might then perform it to warn another of snakes. The communication would now become self-perpetuating in virtue of its general use. What has started as one case of meaning and became a behavioural regularity has now, in virtue of its self-perpetuation, become a convention in Lewis's (1969) sense of that term.

While the communication may be maintained as a convention it may nevertheless evolve in form. The original communication was largely iconic but that is not a necessary feature for its continuation although it may help its establishment. By gradual evolution a non-iconic communication may become established. The tribesmen might in time come to warn each other of the presence of snakes by saying *snakes*.

The example cited shows how, in principle, intention-dependent communication might be established. So far only whole utterance-types have been discussed. Nothing has been said to show how a semantically based system of communication might be established from these beginnings. Grice (1968), Schiffer (1972), and Bennett (1976) have attempted to lay the philosophical foundations for this task. My purpose is not to pursue these arguments but rather to trace a developmental system of communication that begins as intention-dependent communication, somewhat in the manner of the mythical tribe, and becomes a semantically based system. The comparison with the mythical tribe is a limited one for there is an asymmetry in any communication between a child and an adult: the adult knows a conventional language for communicating with others and the child does not know this language. But the comparison is not without content for it is only through the establishment of communicative conventions with one, or at most a few, interlocutors that a child can be inducted into the conventions of a community of speakers.

1.2 The development of intentions

How might the infant begin to behave intentionally? From the earliest months many of the infant's actions and utterances will have the effect of systematically initiating some specific action on the part of his or her caretakers. It obviously does not follow that the behaviour was intended to produce this effect. Nevertheless, in many situations adults readily impute intentions to the behaviour of their infants (Bruner, 1975a; Ninio & Bruner, 1978; Snow, 1977a). By consistently responding to an infant's behaviour as if it was intentional behaviour the adult effectively makes a self-fulfilling prophecy; a contingent relation is established between infant behaviour and adult response and gradually the infant can come to learn this contingent relation between his or her own behaviour and the responses of adults to this behaviour and, having learnt the contingent relation, use this knowledge in order to produce the adult response. When that happens the infant is behaving intentionally.

For at least some behaviours the imputing of intent on the part of the caretaker seems to have a systematic relationship to the infant's innate repertoire of behaviour. Wolff (1969) has shown that certain patterns of crying are consistently interpreted as having particular meanings. Thus, the imputing of intent is not a random interpretation of the infant's behaviour. But neither, as Richards (1974) has pointed out, is it simply a matter of putting inevitable labels on behaviour. To understand the meanings conferred on an infant's activities we need some analysis of the dynamics of social interaction between caretaker and infant. The problem of the development of intentional communicative behaviour is a problem of how the accomplishment of social interaction is managed by the dyad of infant and caretaker and how the infant gradually achieves some intentional control within the dyad.

Recognition of the infant's attempts at communication is subject to a number of interpretative problems. Ryan (1974: 206) describes four kinds of difficulties adults experience when trying to understand young children:

(1) difficulty due to the fact that the child makes noises with no speech-like characteristics at all, such that adults would not readily say she was even

trying to speak, (2) difficulty due to the fact that the child's noises are not recognisably part of the adult vocabulary, but that she makes (utters) them in such a way that she would be described as trying to speak, (3) difficulty due to the fact that a child utters a recognisable standard word but what she means by uttering it is unclear, (4) difficulty due to the unconventional reference with which a child uses a standard word.

Ryan points out that various clues may help the adult in understanding the child. She instances three sorts of interpretative clue: aspects of the utterance such as intonation; accompaniments of the utterance such as pointing, searching, and playing; and circumstances of the utterance such as the presence or absence of particular objects or people and the events preceding the utterance.

The child's attempts to communicate can thus be understood in wider terms than the particular words the child uses. In many cases context and prosody will serve as interpretative clues to the child's intention (as they frequently do to adult intentions also). Some utterances will still remain uninterpretable. There will be cases where an utterance is made without any intention – it is just noise. There will be cases where the child intends to communicate something but the attempted communication fails because the adult fails to understand the intention of the child. These cases will be important from the child's point of view because communication is not just a matter of uttering with some intention but a matter of uttering in such a way that the intention is recognizable. For effective communication by the child intentions must be expressed in such a way that the audience will recognize the intention, and failure of an intended communication helps to establish the limits of an intention's legitimate expression. There will be further cases where the child attempts to communicate something and the adult recognizes the child's intention but refuses to act on this recognition and demands that the child produce a "better" attempt at communicating the particular intention. In these cases the adult is leading the child towards a more conventional means of expressing particular intentions by continually raising the criterion for an appropriate adult response.

The above is no more than a rough sketch of how communication begins – a form of orientation to the task I intend to pursue. The basis of language development is the establishment of intentional communication with another person. Communication does not necessarily depend on using words or on understanding the structure of language, although it may be greatly facilitated by these developments. The intention to communicate with another person develops with the recognition that vocalizations can be used to affect the behaviour of others. There are different ways in which one can affect another's behaviour and therefore different uses to which vocal resources can be put. It follows that separate achievements of intentionality may be required for these different communicative behaviours. These achievements will themselves be the outcome of particular patterns of social and cognitive development. In what follows I shall discuss the antecedents of intentional communicative behaviour in cases where the relevant data are available. The main task, however, is to describe and explain the changes in intentional vocal communication between the ages of 1 and 2 years.

2

The psychology of language development

2.0 Trends in the study of language development

The recent concerns of child language research are best understood in the context of the revolution in linguistics initiated by Chomsky (1957). Chomsky's concern was to give an account of the syntactic structure of language. Previous accounts of the syntax of language had been largely distributional in nature (see Hockett, 1958, for a review of these accounts). Chomsky argued that languages have a "deep structure" from which the actual sentences we speak and hear are generated. The ordinary grammatical structure of a sentence – its "surface structure" – is generated from the sentence's deep structure by a series of transformations of that deep structure. Chomsky advanced many arguments for favouring such a system of syntax. As an illustration of its advantages consider sentences such as

1. The dog bit the cat
2. The cat was bitten by the dog

which seem to have the same meaning and yet apparently have different grammatical structures. In transformational grammar such sentences have the same deep structure and the different surface structures are accounted for by the application of different rules of transformation to that deep structure. On the other hand sentences that have the same surface structure can have very different meanings. Consider the ambiguous sentences

3. They are eating apples
4. The police were ordered to stop drinking after midnight.

The different meanings which these sentences can have is accounted for by the fact that the same surface structure can result from two different deep structures. The interpretation of 'they are eating apples' that implies mastication derives from a different deep structure than the interpretation that implies identification of a type of apple. It is merely a coincidence that the two interpretations can share a common surface structure. As it is only the outline of Chomsky's proposals that are of interest, the details of the relationship between deep and surface structure will not be pursued here.

Influenced by Chomsky's arguments that syntax was best understood in terms of a transformational grammar and by his polemical and widely accepted attack (Chomsky, 1959) on the views of language learning advanced by Skinner (1957), studies of language development began to attempt to characterize and explain the grammar of children's language.

The earliest of these were longitudinal studies of a small number (typically three) of children (Braine, 1963; Brown & Fraser, 1963; Miller & Ervin, 1964). In varying degrees these studies attempted to do two things: to describe the child's progressive acquisition of grammatical structures and to discover the rules that the child was presumed to use to generate such utterances. Menyuk (1963) and McNeill (1966) both attempted to use phrase-structure rules and transformations, as proposed by Chomsky, to describe how children's utterances are generated. However, the assumption of psychologists that transformational grammar could function as a model of speech production was soon called into question. The basic question at issue was the following: given that transformational grammar is a theoretical specification of the structure of language, is there any sense in which the rules of transformational grammar are used by speakers in producing or in understanding utterances?

The negative evidence began with Fodor and Garrett (1966) in their review of studies of language comprehension by adults. The debate continued at a more conceptual level in the articles in Hook (1969). Bloom (1970) and Schlesinger (1971) awakened the world of language development. Gradually a reevaluation of the earlier naive acceptance of transformational grammar as a psychological model began. The reverberations affected linguistics, psychology and the original theory itself. The results have been too widespread to be traced here but two related developments in linguistics and psychology are of particular importance in understanding the reorientation of language development studies that followed.

Within linguistics it soon became apparent that even if the general outline of Chomsky's proposals was to be accepted the details would have to be revised. In particular there would have to be more room for semantics in deep structure. To illustrate these developments consider the following unacceptable sentences

*5. A hammer broke the glass with a chisel (Fillmore, 1968: 22)

*6. I am halfway finished with writing my dissertation, which weighs five pounds (McCawley, 1968: 131).

Sentence 5 is anomalous (on its literal interpretation) because the verb 'break', when used transitively with an instrumental phrase, requires an animate agent, and sentence 6 is anomalous because the statement contained in the relative clause presupposes the existence of a completed dissertation. The anomaly of these sentences has nothing to do with their syntax and the sentences would thus be perfectly well-formed in the original theory advanced by Chomsky (1957, 1965). The only way in which standard transformational grammar could deny such sentences the status of legitimate sentences was by *ad hoc* revision of the theory. As the number of anomalies grew so did the number of *ad hoc* revisions necessary. The alternative to this unsatisfactory state of affairs was some fundamental revision of the theory. This came in the form of a revised conception of the nature of the deep structure of language. Various proposals (e.g. Fillmore, 1968; Lakoff, 1971; McCawley, 1968; Ross, 1970) were made that the purely syntactic deep structure of transformational grammar be replaced by a more semantically based deep structure. The most influential of the proposed revisions was Fillmore's (1968) case grammar and its application to language development will be considered in 2.1.1.

The first related shift of theoretical emphasis in language development was proposed by Schlesinger (1971). He suggested that the underlying structure of children's speech is not syntactic but semantic in nature and reflects the way the child perceives the world. While approaches based on transformational grammar had regarded the child as having innate syntactic rules, Schlesinger regarded the child as having innate cognitive capacities, which determine the conceptual categorization of reality. These concepts in turn determine the nature of the semantic concepts of language. Schlesinger proposed that cognition and semantics alike encode a world of agents, actions, objects, possessors-of-objects, locations-of-objects, and so on. The link between cognition and language is provided by a series of "realization rules", which children infer by observing how adults express salient concepts in speech. The child is able to map his or her concepts on to the adult expression of these concepts because the common situation between child and adult provides an interpretative clue to the meaning of adult utterances.

Although Schlesinger's proposals were closely related to the general framework of transformational grammar his theory took the first step towards what was to become a popular semantically based theory of language development. Schlesinger's argument still contained the idea that language structure is determined by innate capacities but the innateness had shifted from grammar to cognition. In Schlesinger's theory grammar is learnt, and moreover grammar is essentially a semantically based system. The next step was to dispel innate ideas altogether. A considerable amount of work on early cognitive development, principally that of Piaget (e.g. 1937), suggested that the conceptual categorization of reality develops gradually during the first two years of life as a result of a child's active interaction with the environment. The concepts that characterize the achievements of sensorimotor intelligence in Piaget's theory are the same concepts that are expressed in the earliest two-word utterances. Edwards (1973) gives the most detailed account of the relationship between the concepts of sensorimotor intelligence and the semantic relations expressed in two-word utterances. Brown (1973: 200) summed up a growing consensus:

The first sentences express the construction of reality which is the terminal achievement of sensorimotor intelligence. What has been acquired on the plane of motor intelligence (the permanence of form and substance of immediate objects) and the structure of immediate space and time does not need to be formed all over again on the plane of representation. Representation starts with just those meanings that are most available to it, propositions about action schemas involving agents and objects, assertions of non-existence, recurrence, location and so on.

2.1 One-word utterances

Up to this point most studies of language development had concentrated on the development of grammatical structure in children's language and the principal object of study had consequently been the emergence of two-word utterances in speech. However, before two-word utterances begin to be spoken some time between the ages of 18 and 24 months, most children will have spent several months speaking one word at a time. Although largely neglected in the initial wave of Chomsky-inspired studies of language development the shift of interest to the semantics of children's utterances resulted in several new accounts of this earlier phase of language development.

2.1.1 The "structure" of one-word utterances

Chomsky's lasting influence on the study of language has been the continued centrality of considerations of language structure. So strong has been the influence that structural considerations have been extended to one-word speech, a paradox that a shift of interest to the semantics of utterances has, if anything, accentuated.

McNeill (1970) was among the first to offer a theoretical account of one-word speech. Following Chomsky (1965), McNeill argued that knowledge of basic syntactic relations is innate and that children's experience with language merely provides the children with information for learning the relevant surface structures of their native tongues. McNeill argued that single-word utterances have the underlying representation of a full sentence but that only one element of this underlying structure is realized in the surface structure. This interpretation was disputed by Bloom (1973) and by Dore (1975). Bloom pointed out that children are not constrained to utter only one word at a time; utterances longer than one word occur but they do not contain more than one meaningful element. Bloom also argued that when children do begin to produce words in combination they initially produce successive single-word utterances in which each word relates to some aspect of the same situation, each word has a similar prosodic contour with a definite pause between words, and there is little, if any, constraint on word order. This suggests that children do not, at the one-word stage, know anything about syntax. Children utter one word at a time because they have not yet learnt any rules for combining words. Dore disputed McNeill's interpretation on somewhat different grounds. He argued that the issue of one-word utterances could more readily be resolved if children's pragmatic intentions in using words to communicate were the starting-point of study. Dore argued that the communicative functions of language are learnt first and these are later "grammaticalized" as children learn semantic and syntactic structures. (Dore's account of this process will be considered in 2.1.3.)

The most detailed consideration of the "structure" of one-word utterances has been presented by Greenfield and Smith (1976). They argue that case grammar, as proposed by Fillmore (1968) and by Chafe (1970), provides a useful framework for understanding language development. In case grammar the central element in a sentence is the verb, and nouns, or noun-phrases, are associated with the verb in a particular "case" relationship, which relationship is determined by the verb. The objections raised above to

*5. A hammer broke the glass with a chisel

was that the verb 'break', when used transitively with an instrumental phrase, requires an animate noun, or, in Fillmore's terms, the Agentive case. Fillmore (1968: 24–5) introduces an initial taxonomy of cases with the following distinctly psychological preface:

The case notions comprise a set of universal, presumably innate, concepts which identify certain types of judgements human beings are capable of making about the events that are going on around them, judgements about such matters as who did it, who it happened to, and what got changed. The cases that appear to be needed include:

Agentive (A), the case of the typically animate perceived instigator of the action identified by the verb.

Instrumental (I), the case of the inanimate force or object causally involved in the action or state identified by the verb.

Dative (D), the case of the animate being affected by the state or action identified by the verb.

Factitive (F), the case of the object or being resulting from the action or state identified by the verb, or understood as a part of the meaning of the verb.

Locative (L), the case which identifies the location or spatial orientation of the state or action identified by the verb.

Objective (O), the semantically most neutral case, the case of anything representable by a noun whose role in the action or state identified by the verb is identified by the semantic interpretation of the verb itself; conceivably the concept should be limited to things which are affected by the action or state identified by the verb. The term is not to be confused with the notion of direct object, nor with the name of the surface case synonymous with accusative.

In order to apply case grammar to language development Greenfield and Smith propose a number of modifications of previous conceptions of the relation between grammatical structure and utterances.

Greenfield and Smith point out that the base structure of the grammar proposed by Bloom (1970), and other grammars similarly based on transformational theory, are richer than any surface string actually uttered by the child. Consequently it is necessary to invoke "deletion rules" to account for the simpler surface structure. However, these rules must be dropped from the grammar as the child's utterances get longer. Such a theory posits an unlikely developmental sequence of more complex stages before simpler ones and leads to the *reductio ad absurdum* that the most complex deletion rules are required for one-word utterances. Consequently Greenfield and Smith propose that base structure be redefined so that:

at the outset of language development, the base structure is not composed of words but consists of a structured perception of real (or imagined) entities and relations. The surface string may be thought of as a partial verbal realization of a nonverbal base. With this formulation, we need not be bothered by the fact that two-word utterances, describing the Action of an Agent upon an Object sometimes encode the Agent and Action, sometimes the Action and Object, and sometimes the Agent and Object, but never all three, as Bloom (1970) and others report. If the base structure is a perceptual–cognitive structure of ongoing events, then the base will not be *linguistically* more complex than the surface, although it may be *cognitively* more complex. (1976: 63)

They thus propose that language and cognition share the same underlying structure. The case grammar categories of Agent, Action, Location, etc. are, they argue, basic cognitive categories of experience – "situations are structured like sentences on a cognitive level" (1976: 54) – and utterances relate to these basic categories in the following way:

The single-word utterance is a functional part of the cognitive organization of a particular referential situation...Semantic function [indicates] the structural point at which the child's word fits into the cognitive structure of a given event. In claiming that the word is part of the cognitive structure of an event, we are saying something about *how* nonverbal cognitive organization is used in the language learning process.

(1976: 214)

In what way are one-word utterances "a functional part of a particular referential situation"? Greenfield and Smith seem committed to the view that the child, when speaking a one-word utterance, has cognitively organized a more complex message of which the utterance is only a partial realization. They argue as follows:

The child's gestures and orientation, particularly pointing and reaching, indicate important elements of the situation...we assume that, if a child is pointing to a fan, the fan is an element of the message the child wishes to convey, even though the child may not use the word *fan*.

(1976: 45)

It is a common observation that the communicative force of children's utterances is often readily intelligible when the utterances are judged in the context of their occurrence. Using the context of the utterance as an interpretative clue to a child's meaning is now a common strategy of research on child language. However, Greenfield and Smith are unique in their proposal that contextual features should be treated as *elements of the message* in the sense that these features are structural components of a more complexly ordered deep structure. Their claim does not merely make the important point that the meaning of an utterance must be judged in context but suggests that children's utterances have an underlying generative structure that makes elements of the situation elements of the message. In effect the proposal is that what are generally regarded as the pragmatics of messages be incorporated into a generative model of the semantics of messages. Greenfield and Smith offer no particular justification for this radical proposal. The proposal seems, in fact, to be a consequence of their adoption of an interpretative framework (case grammar) that requires that semantic content be specified by elements in a formal relationship in a deep structure. As a one-word utterance provides only one element the other must apparently be found elsewhere.

The attraction of applying case grammar to one-word speech is that it provides a potential means of semantic categorization in terms that bear a striking isomorphism to the child's conceptual organization of the world. However, the functional identification of semantic and cognitive structures is achieved only by a procrustean redefinition of the concept of base structure and by an equally procrustean reinterpretation of the role of the context of utterances. (On this issue see Dore, 1979.) The merits of the system of categorization proposed by Greenfield and Smith will be discussed in 4.8.2 where their system will be compared with the system of categorization proposed in this book.

In summary, neither McNeill (1970) nor Greenfield and Smith (1976) present a plausible case that one-word utterances exhibit deep structure, however that concept be defined. The following section discusses two studies, Bloom's (1973) and Nelson's (1973), which attempt to trace the developmental course from one-word utterances to structured utterances without assuming that one-word utterances have a deep structure.

2.1.2 *The studies of Bloom and of Nelson*

Bloom's account of one-word speech is based on a diary study of her daughter, Allison. The central issue to which Bloom addresses herself is why children use only one word at a time. She proposes that there are linguistic and psychological limitations which account for this. By 'linguistic limitations' Bloom means that children do not have an innate knowledge of grammar. By 'psychological limitations' Bloom means that language is learnt "as a linguistic coding of developmentally prior conceptual representations of experience" (1973: 16) and that the nature of conceptual representation is such that syntax is not learnt till about the end of the sensorimotor period. Bloom argues as follows.

Children's utterances consist of words of two sorts during the one-word stage: substance words and function words. Substance words are words that name objects, whereas function words do not name objects but refer to the functions that a variety of objects may perform. Bloom argues that substance words are initially "loosely associated" with an object but that they later achieve the status of being a name for the object. This development, Bloom argues, is dependent on the development of Stage VI of object permanence. Bloom provides no empirical support for this proposition; the argument resting speculatively on the coincidence of age of appearance of naming in Allison and the normal age of achieving Stage VI of object permanence in Piaget's theory of sensorimotor development. Corrigan (1978) has pointed out that the problem of tracing any relationship between Stage VI of object permanence and language development is considerable as the child is typically in a global Stage VI for a period of six months. It is therefore necessary to narrow the specification on the cognitive side of the relationship before useful predictions can be made and tested about any relationship between object permanence and language development. Bloom argues that, with the development of object permanence, objects can now be mentally represented by the child independently of their perceived schemes. An object's name may now be combined with a word for some other part of a scheme in which the object is perceived and structured utterances will begin to appear in the child's speech. Structured utterances are initially of two sorts. The first sort involves the combination of a function and a substance word (e.g. *more* and *ball*). In such utterances the function word determines the semantic–syntactic relationship (e.g. *more*, uttered with the name of an object, signals recurrence). In the second sort two substance words co-occur and Bloom offers a more abstract analysis. She argues that, before structured utterances develop, one-word utterances occur as references to successive aspects of a single event. The relations between the different aspects of the whole event lead to the development of similar relations at the level of language. Thus, a child might form conceptual categories of agent, possessor, object-acted-upon, and so on. These conceptual categories organize the child's experience of events. As the child uses words in relation to these events the words begin to assume semantic significance relative to each other. When the child realizes that different words can be used to express the same meaning relation the child has the basis for formulating a linguistic category. Thus, *mummy*, *daddy*, *doggie*, might all be used to express the concept of agent, thus aiding the formulation of the linguistic concept of Agent. However, the linguistic categories that are derived from the coneptual representation of experience must consist of a good deal more than recasting concepts such as agent as a semantic category and then as a syntactic category (subject-of-a-sentence), for Bloom argues that an utterance such as *mommy pigtail* is to be understood as *mommy [verb (me)] pigtail* with the verb "deleted" (1973: 133–4). It is not at all clear what sort of linguistic induction on the child's part can account for the absent presence of a linguistic relation. As Greenfield and Smith (1976) have argued, such an account posits the unlikely developmental sequence of using a more complex rule-system for two-word utterances than for three- or four-word utterances, as in these latter utterances the verb will be specified in the surface structure and the child can now dispense with the deletion rule.

We now turn to Bloom's account of function and substance words in one-word speech itself. Utterances such as *more*, *away*, *no*, *stop*, are examples of function words cited by Bloom. Function words occurred with a high frequency in Allison's early speech and they persisted over time unlike substance words, which sometimes were used for a short time and then disappeared from the child's vocabulary. Bloom states that function words were identified on the basis of their "frequency, endurance, and referential function" (1973: 84–5). This raises the question of which criterion (frequency, endurance, or referential function) is being used to identify a function word. The question is somewhat jejune, as none of the criteria is, in any case, adequate. Whereas it may (or may not, see Corrigan, 1978) be an empirical fact that function words are more frequent and more enduring than substance words in one-word speech, this is merely a contingent observation and cannot be a criterion of identification, as a word's status in no way depends upon its frequency of use or its endurance. The only remaining criterion for identification is referential function. However, it is undoubtedly misleading to speak of the referential function of many of Bloom's function words as they do not *refer* to anything but rather fulfil a variety of communicative functions such as requesting or describing (*more*), ordering or protesting (*away*, *stop*) and refusing (*no*).

The major difficulty with Bloom's method is that the child's utterances are categorized in terms that bear no obvious relevance to the child's use of these utterances or to the intention with which a child might have made an utterance. The difficulty is particularly clear in Bloom's treatment of substance words. A substance word is a word that makes reference to an object. However, Bloom fails to distinguish between words that refer to objects and words that the child uses to refer to objects, thus leading her to categorize a word as a substance word on the basis of its grammatical form in adult language rather than its function in the child's language. (The disadvantages of such an approach have already been considered in Chapter 1.) The treatment of function words is similarly unsatisfactory. No plausible argument is presented that the motley class of function words is a class with any psychological reality for the child. In summary, the distinction between substance and function words is not grounded in any behavioural or cognitive facts that relate to the child's linguistic or communicative abilities.

Similar problems attach to Nelson's (1973) study. In contrast to Bloom's diary study this study included a sample of 18 children. However, the method of data collection leads to some immediate problems. The children's speech was not studied directly but mothers' records of the children's speech were used. This strategy is open to the obvious difficulty that there may be considerable differences between mothers in what is regarded as a "word". Differences between children are vitiated by possible differential reporting. A further feature of Nelson's study is that, in interpreting how a word was used by a child, only the first reported use of a word was considered. Several potential problems attach to this: the way in which a word is used may change over time – this is ignored by Nelson's study; nonstandard usage may be ignored by parents, thus biasing reports in the direction of conventional usage; by ignoring frequency of use, the relative importance of some aspect of a child's use of language may be distorted.

The aim of Nelson's study was to describe the process involved in moving from single-word utterances to longer utterances. In order to do this both the grammatical form and the semantic content of the children's single-word utterances were studied. As already stated there are considerable methodological difficulties attached to classifying children's utterances according to grammatical form. The concepts of noun, verb, or adjective are concepts that can only be applied to words on the basis of their grammatical function in sentences. These concepts are therefore inappropriate for the analysis of children's one-word speech as was pointed out by Dewey (1894). Nelson assigned words to a particular form-category on the basis of "the grammatical function the unit would take on in a fully wrought sentence" (1974: 11). This is tantamount to assuming that each utterance of a child can be readily identified in such terms and barely misses (if it does) assuming that children are learning nouns, verbs, and adjectives (or nominals, action words, and modifiers as Nelson calls them). An example from Nelson's data illustrates the problem: *door* was classified as an action word because it was used as a request to open the door. This is doubly unsatisfactory: it flies in the face of the avowed method ("the grammatical function the unit would take on in a fully wrought sentence") and it confuses pragmatics with grammar. The child's behaviour was that of making a request. This is the behaviour he or she has learnt to perform in order to enlist other people's aid and he or she uses a particular utterance (*door* in this case) in order to request. What is of interest in describing the processes involved in one-word speech is what behaviours the child engages in when using words and what inferences about the cognitive organization of language can be made on the basis of these behaviours. If the form of adult language is imposed on the child's language from the beginning than we shall always have homunculus theories of language development.

2.1.3 *One-word utterances as speech-acts*

Utterances have both a structure and a function. At minimum there are facts about how a language is used as well as facts about how it is structured. It is also possible, indeed likely, that each set of facts can only be fully understood in relation to the other. If structure and function interrelate in the process of language development then more direct attention to the functions of language is necessary than is evident in any of the studies reviewed above.

It is only comparatively recently that any attention has been paid to developing a framework within which language use can be studied. The need for such a framework was argued for by

Campbell and Wales (1970), Habermas (1970) and Ryan (1974) among others. These authors argued that a theory of language development has to account not only for the development of grammar but also for the development of communicative skills that are at least as essential to speaking and understanding as is an ability to generate syntactic utterances. The pioneering studies in this area are those of Bates, Camaioni, and Volterra (1975), Bruner (1975a, 1975b), Dore (1973) and Halliday (1975). The novelty of these studies is twofold: they make language use the primary object of study in contrast to the more structurally oriented studies already discussed and they place language development within the more general context of communicative development. The central argument advanced by this research is that communication between adult and child establishes many of the conventions that underlie the use of language, and that language development is facilitated by earlier forms of social interaction in that language explicitly encodes routines, or aspects of routines, with which the child is already familiar. The theoretical framework to which many of these accounts have turned is that of speech-act theory as advanced by Austin (1962) and by Searle (1969).

In introducing the concept of a speech-act, Austin pointed out that many philosophical accounts of language concentrated exclusively on the descriptive use of language and failed to give any adequate account of the wide variety of non-descriptive uses of language – for example, promising, warning, commanding, requesting, criticizing, apologizing, challenging, censuring, approving, greeting – that are not references to an event but rather constitute an event in themselves. While it has often been recognized that language has such "instrumental functions" (e.g. Buhler, 1934; Cassirer, 1923; Saussure, 1916) a careful analysis of these functions was lacking until Austin's work. Austin's analysis concentrated on two main themes: the social interactive conditions ("felicity conditions") that attend the successful performance of any particular speech-act, and the different acts that speakers perform in speaking an utterance, namely: locutionary, illocutionary, and perlocutionary acts. The locutionary act consists in uttering certain words. The illocutionary act consists in (*eo ipso*) performing a particular speech-act (describing, warning, etc.) in uttering these words. The perlocutionary act consists in producing certain consequential effects upon the thoughts, feelings, or behaviour of one's audience (which effect may be planned or unplanned).

Searle's (1969) version of speech-act theory is somewhat different from Austin's. Searle argues that, in speaking, speakers essentially do three things: they utter words (utterance acts); in doing so they generally refer to some thing, event, etc. (propositional acts); in doing so they perform some particular speech-act (illocutionary acts). Searle thus ignores the perlocutionary acts of Austin's theory and subdivides Austin's locutionary acts into utterance acts and propositional acts. Like Austin, Searle emphasizes that the different acts are not separate things that speakers do in speaking but are, in general, a necessary part of each utterance.[1] Unlike Austin, Searle attempts to give an account of how an utterance is recognized as a speech-act of a particular sort. (Austin is content to point to the common-sense fact that we do recognize different speech-acts as such.) To recognize which speech-act is being performed Searle argues that one must understand what the speaker's intentions were in speaking the utterance. But, Searle argues, intentions do not operate independently of the speaker's utterance – speakers must intend that their intentions will be recognized in virtue of their conformity to rules governing the use of linguistic elements (and the audience, for their part, must be capable of recognizing that a speaker is thus conforming).

The application of speech-act theory to language development is not an entirely straightforward affair. On Searle's account communicative intentions and grammatical structure form a closely knit system: the grammatical structure of utterances is the primary means by which speakers reveal their intentions and the primary means by which listeners discover what the speaker's intentions are. There are inherent problems in applying such a model to language development (see 1.1 above) and evidence that the model is inadequate (Shatz, 1978). In particular, grammatical structure cannot serve as a means of conveying intentions for a child who has not yet learnt these structures. If speech-act theory is to have

---

[1] Not all speech-acts have propositional content; for example: *hallo, ouch, thank you*.

application to language development the relation between communicative intentions and grammatical structure must itself be the object of study. Dore (1973) was among the first to propose a speech-act analysis of children's utterances. In a study of two children during the time they spoke one-word utterances, Dore described a variety of "primitive speech-acts" – labelling, repeating, answering, requesting, calling, greeting, protesting, practising – which the children carried out with single words. Dore argues that one-word utterances were used to express a communicative intention of some sort, which intention was indicated by the context and the prosody of the child's utterance. Following Searle's distinction between the propositional content and the illocutionary force of an utterance, Dore regards the words the children used as "rudimentary referring expressions" and the prosody of the utterance as the "primitive force indicating device". Thus, Dore argues that one-word utterances are a kind of first-order version of adult-type speech-acts. In order to explain the transition to grammatically structured utterances Dore proposes that two basic linguistic skills, reference and predication, are innate linguistic skills, which operate to transform "rudimentary referring expressions" into "rudimentary propositions" and thus bring the child's utterances more closely into line with adult-type utterances. The unfolding of the innate linguistic skills of reference and predication leads to the development of grammatically structured two-word utterances and thus to the development of conventional speech-acts. Language development as envisaged by Dore is represented in Figure 1.

Dore's contention that reference and predication are innate linguistic skills was based on his belief that it does not seem possible that a child could learn what a referring expression is or what predication is, and these concepts must, in consequence, be innate. The absurdity of invoking innateness on such grounds has been pointed out by Lieven and McShane (1978). The issue of how the concepts of reference and predication are mastered and how they relate to the development of grammar is one to which Dore (1978) has, however, returned with a different proposal. His later argument is that reference can only be explained by allowing that the child

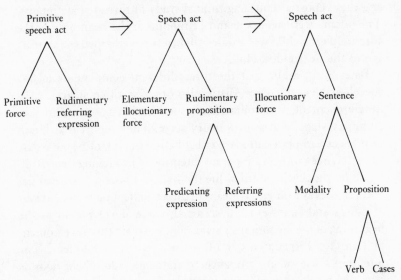

Figure 1. The development of speech-acts as envisaged by Dore (1975: 35–6)

forms a specific "designation hypothesis" concerning reference. This hypothesis allows the child to

come to know that a linguistic category signalled by a sound-sequence represents a concept independently (1) of the concept's own representation of objects, events, etc. (a sensorimotor schema perhaps); (2) of the defining characteristics of the concept; and (3) of its active involvement with instances of the concept. (1978: 96)

Dore does not explain how it is that a child might form a "designation hypothesis". In the absence of a specification of the conditions that might facilitate such a hypothesis the proposal that it accounts for the development of reference is vacuous. But, regardless of the fact that the solution to the problem of the development of grammatical structure is deficient, Dore's attempt to use speech-act theory as a framework for language development helped to introduce a new perspective to studies of language development.

Bates *et al.* (1975) have also used speech-act theory as a framework for analysing the development of communication. They were concerned to trace the developmental course of speech-acts and they report a semi-longitudinal study of three female infants. The infants were aged 2, 6 and 12 months at the beginning of the study and each child was studied till her age overlapped the starting age of the next oldest child.

Bates *et al.* argue that the three different components of any speech-act identified by Austin also describe three stages in the development of communication: a perlocutionary stage, an illocutionary stage, and a locutionary stage. They report that infant utterances had perlocutionary effect before the infant began to use her utterances with any apparent intention of producing that effect. By about the tenth month of life their subject became aware of her vocal signals as a potential means of directly affecting the behaviour of others and Bates *et al.* describe this new development as the beginning of the illocutionary stage. They explain this development in terms of Piaget's theory of sensorimotor development. The intentional use of an utterance to influence adult behaviour is regarded by Bates *et al.* as an instance of means–end behaviour (a proposal also advanced by Sugarman-Bell, 1978). The behaviour appeared contemporaneously with other means–end behaviours that characterize Stage V of sensorimotor development in Piaget's theory. Bates *et al.* thus regard the illocutionary stage of language development as part of Stage V of sensorimotor development.

On similar grounds the achievement of Stage VI of sensorimotor development and the locutionary stage of language development are linked. In Piaget's theory Stage VI is characterized by the development of symbolic behaviour and a capacity for internal representation. Bates *et al.* argue that these Stage VI developments lead to the locutionary stage of language development and the replacement of "sensorimotor performatives" (i.e. illocutionary stage utterances) by "words with symbolic value" (1975: 220).

The value of stages of sensorimotor development as explanations of language development rests entirely on causation being deduced from correlation. This suspect enterprise is further weakened by the particular difficulties that attach to any interpretation of Stage VI of sensorimotor development (see 2.2.7) and the nature of the evidence that Bates *et al.* present. The latter difficulty – the nature of the evidence presented – is due to the fact that Bates *et al.* offer no systematic data on the course of language development; their evidence consists entirely of selective anecdotes.

Within their stage model of language development Bates *et al.*
confined their observations to two speech-acts: declaratives[2] and
imperatives. They argue that the communicative precursors to
declaratives are the child's attempts to regulate the attention of
another, defining the illocutionary stage proto-declarative as "a
preverbal effort to direct the adult's attention to some event or
object in the world" (1975: 208). Following Parisi and Antinucci
(1973) they regard the declarative as:

a particular kind of imperative which commands the unique epistemic act
of "assuming" some proposition...[it is] a command for the listener to
attend to or assume some piece of information.   (1975: 208)

This definition of the declarative allows a synthesis of preverbal
means of commanding attention and declarative utterances. The
synthesis is procrustean. The declarative has none of the characteristics of an imperative, a term that identifies a particular sort of
speech-act in contrast to other speech-acts such as declaratives.
Consequently there is little justification for regarding declaratives
as imperatives of any kind. This criticism is not intended to deny
a possible relationship between joint attention and declaratives.
Werner and Kaplan (1963) and Bruner (1975a, 1975b) have argued
for just such a developmental relationship, and Olson (1970) and
Rommetveit (1974) have argued that joint attention is an important
factor in understanding the normal adult use of declarative
utterances. The role of joint attention in language development will
be returned to in 2.2.5.

In their discussion of imperatives Bates *et al.* define the
illocutionary stage proto-imperative as: "the child's intentional use
of the listener as the agent or tool in achieving some end" (1975:
208). They found that they could identify imperative vocalizations,
which were used by the child in order to obtain the listener's aid.
Their observation in this context is supported by the intonation
of infant utterances and the interpretation of such intonation by
adults. Tonkova-Yampol'skaya (1969) found that intonation
patterns that correspond to adult intonation are present by the end
of the first year. Adults can reliably distinguish such patterns in
children's utterances (Menyuk & Bernholtz, 1969) and will

---

[2] 'Declarative' as used by Bates *et al.* is more or less synonymous with the term 'statement'
in this book.

consistently interpret differences in intonation as signalling different requirements by the child (Ricks, 1971, 1975). The continuity from proto-imperative to imperative is unproblematic as far as function is concerned because no change of function occurs. However, Dore (1978) has objected that the imperative utterances Bates *et al.* regard as requests are not analogous to genuine requests. A "genuine request", according to Dore, requires that:

(a) the communicative intention be an inducement in the listener of a recognition of a complex set of the speaker's internal states;

(b) the proposition contain specifications of the agent, future act, etc.;

(c) its use involve assumptions about the listener's willingness and ability to perform the future act.

While it may be true that some adult requests would fulfil Dore's three conditions, not all adult requests would do so. Even for adult requests the conditions would be unduly restrictive and it seems that they identify a particular complex class of requests rather than "genuine requests". The following is a counterexample to condition (a):

S$_1$: *Pass the hammer please.*

S$_2$: *What do you want it for?*

S$_1$: *Mind your own business.*

As argued in 1.1 the communicative intention necessary in making a request is the speaker's intention that: (i) the hearer should do as requested, (ii) the hearer should be aware of intention (i), and (iii) this awareness should be part of the hearer's reason for doing as requested. A speaker may, of course, intend additional inducements in the hearer of the sort Dore specifies but these are not a necessary condition of requesting.

The following is a counterexample to condition (b):

S: *Salt.*

Condition (c) presents no challenge to the Bates *et al.* account; they attempt to describe how such assumptions achieve linguistic expression.

While it is undoubtedly true that the linguistic and interpersonal form of children's requests is less sophisticated than that of many adult requests, this cannot be a reason for denying children's requests the status of "genuine requests" as Dore argues. A general feature of development is the initial limited ability to use any skill and the subsequent gradual elaboration and sophistication of that skill. Limited abilities are just that: limited, not ungenuine, and a discussion of genuineness is disingenous.

2.1.4 *Halliday's theory of language development*

Halliday (1975) has presented an account of language development which emphasizes the communicative functions of language but which differs from speech-act theory. The empirical basis of Halliday's theory derives from his own observations of his son, Nigel, between the ages of 9 and 24 months.

Halliday's theoretical orientation is that language is a means (*inter alia*) of constructing a social and conceptual framework of the world. The initial uses a child makes of language, Halliday argues, are limited and are largely utilitarian in nature. In using the term 'language' Halliday, unlike many others, does not restrict its application solely to words but uses it to cover any use to which children put their vocal resources. Toward the end of the first year the child's progress, *qua* language, amounts to the discovery that his or her vocal resources can be used to accompany or accomplish interaction with others. The child at this stage does not possess a lexicon; even if a number of phonological forms resembling words are used by the child, they do not have the status of words; they are merely sounds used to accomplish some particular end, sounds which in some cases have been acquired from the environment and so bear a phonological similarity to adult words. Halliday argues that the child's language undergoes a number of "restructurings" leading to changes in the system that the child possesses and finally bringing that system into alignment with the adult system. Such is an outline of Halliday's system. A more detailed discussion follows.

By the end of the first year a child will have learnt that his or her own voice can be used as part of the process of interaction with others. The initial functions that language serves in these interactions Halliday identifies as:

(a) The *instrumental*: the child's demand for objects.

(b) The *regulatory*: the child's demand that another person do something.

The difference between the instrumental and the regulatory functions is specified by Halliday as follows:

In the instrumental the focus is on the goods or services required and it does not matter who provides them, whereas regulatory utterances are directed towards a particular individual, and it is the behaviour of that individual that is to be influenced. (1975: 19)

(c) The *interactional*: utterances such as greeting and attention-getting.

This function, according to Halliday, has a pragmatic element – the need for human contact – but is distinguished from the regulatory function because the meanings are the expression of the interaction itself rather than the demand for it.

(d) The *personal*: described as "expressions of personal feelings, of participation and withdrawal, of interest, pleasure, disgust and so forth" (1975: 20).

These four functions were the first to appear in Nigel's language. They were shortly followed by two other functions, the heuristic and the imaginative. A further function, the *informative*, did not appear till a much later date in Nigel's development.

(e) The *heuristic*: language used to question another about the environment. Its earliest manifestation in Nigel's system was a demand for a name which Halliday says "is the child's way of categorizing the objects of the physical world" (1975: 20).

(f) The *imaginative*: the language which the child uses "for creating a universe of his own, a world initially of pure sound, but which gradually turns into one of story and make-believe and let's-pretend" (1975: 20).

According to Halliday these initial functions are defined "extra-linguistically". That is to say, the child's system and his or her uses of language are coextensive at this stage; there is no level of organization such as a lexicon or syntax intermediate between a function and its expression and the child does not need a specific language, such as English, to express these functions.

This limited system is, Halliday argues, "restructured" by the child. The effect of the restructuring is to impose a lexicon and syntax between the functions that language serves and the means of expressing these functions. In effect the child's language becomes conventionalized – it becomes English rather than any other language. Halliday argues that this change comes about by "the generalization, out of the initial set of developmental functions, of a fundamental distinction between language as doing and language as learning" (1975: 35). This "fundamental distinction" now becomes the organizing principle of the linguistic system (replacing the initial functional principle). The main justifications for arguing for this restructuring are twofold:

(i) Nigel rapidly learnt a large number of words, many of which had no utilitarian use, and shortly afterwards (within a few weeks) began to construct a grammar.

(ii) Within one week of the beginning of (a) Nigel differentiated two uses of language which he distinguished by intonation. *Pragmatic* utterances ("language as doing") had a rising tone and *mathetic* utterances ("language as learning") had a falling tone.

The initial learning of a lexicon Halliday regards as transitional between Phase I and Phase II. He further argues that the functions of Phase I are "combined" to give the new functional principles of Phase II, and he states that it is the learning of a lexicon that "allows for the functions to be combined" (1975: 42). Thus, the functional principles of Phase I are not merely replaced by those of Phase II; they evolve from them by "combination". As an example of this, consider the mathetic function. It is due, primarily, to a combination of the personal and heuristic functions, the personal function contributing attention ("expressions of interest" in the definition above) to some object, and the heuristic function contributing an interest in the object's name. Halliday describes the process as follows:

Nigel begins...by using some external object, typically a picture, as a channel for interaction with others...He then...separates the interactional from the personal element, the former developing into forms of greeting and the latter into 'self' expressions of interest, pleasure and the like. Then, as the split between the self and the environment becomes clearer, the interactional element reappears on a higher level, the attention being focussed on an external object which the other person is required to name...At first this is used only when the object is familiar...typically a picture – and the name already (receptively) known; it then splits into

two meanings one of which is a demand for a new name...The words
that name objects are at the same time being learnt productively, and are
then used in the encoding of expressions of personal interest and
involvement...Thus out of a combination of the personal (self-oriented)
and the heuristic (environment-oriented) functions of Phase I there arises
a generalized non-pragmatic mode of meaning. (1975: 74)

Although the observations of Nigel's behaviour are detailed and
acute, it may be asked if the account offered provides any
compelling evidence for the discontinuity posited between Phase
I and Phase II. There is, to begin with, a considerable lack of clarity
in the processes involved in the transition, particularly in the
process of functional combination which leads to a restructuring
of the child's system. The account is further weakened by the fact
that Halliday's theory and his empirical evidence are not always
in accord. As stated, he interprets the mathetic function of Phase
II as a combination of the personal and heuristic functions of Phase
I. However, an examination of the data (see his Table 1, p. 147,
which presents the expressions used in the various functions in
Phase I and Phase II) reveals that there are no entries for the
heuristic function during Phase I. This must lead to some difficulty
in combining the heuristic and personal functions in order to effect
the transition to Phase II. The problems with Halliday's
interpretation of the heuristic function go further than this. During
particular attentional interactions with a "Phase I child", the
typical adult response to a child's utterances may be to name
objects. This does not necessarily mean that the child's utterance
was a request for a name (he or she will not, of course, possess the
conventional means of asking for a name at this stage). The child
may merely have indicated attention or, if the utterance was a
request of some sort, it could more neutrally be interpreted as a
request for a response by the adult rather than a request for a *name*.
To regard the heuristic function as a demand for a name is to regard
it as a function that is already linguistically defined, at least
receptively. It is precisely this linguistic feature which is absent in
all other Phase I functions and whose absence defines the functions
as Phase I functions.

In Halliday's study the most compelling fact in need of

explanation is that Nigel's vocabulary increased suddenly at $16\frac{1}{2}$ months, the majority of the new words being names for objects (75 per cent by Halliday's estimate). This development Halliday regards as transitional between Phase I and Phase II and it results in a functional reorganization of the child's system into mathetic and pragmatic functions. However, to argue, as Halliday does, that the child restructures his understanding of language in such a way that one result of the restructuring is the postulation of a function (the mathetic), which describes the phenomenon observed (the learning of names), is mere nominalism unless a coherent account of the process of restructuring itself is offered. This account Halliday does not provide.

Further difficulties arise when Halliday's conception of the mathetic function is considered in more detail. He regards this function, of which naming is the first exemplar, as the use of language to learn about the environment. It is unclear what naming teaches the child about the environment. The realization that things have names is not a discovery about the environment but a discovery about the relationship between language and the environment. Halliday regards this relationship as unproblematic in itself – things have names because that is the way the world is. However, more considered views of the concept of naming (Nelson, 1974; Piaget, 1945; Werner & Kaplan, 1963) have seen it necessary to explain how the child comes to understand what the conceptual relationship is between names and objects. This issue will be discussed in more detail in the sections from 2.2 onwards.

Halliday's treatment of the subsequent development of the language system is subject to similar difficulties. Shortly after the onset of naming, structured utterances began to appear in Nigel's speech. Halliday argues that the structures and the vocabulary are at first functionally specific. Subsequently the utterances became "functionally derestricted" (1975: 47). In order to explain this development Halliday postulates a further restructuring of the linguistic system, which takes place by "a recasting of the concept of 'function' on to a more abstract plane so that all expressions become, in effect, plurifunctional" (1975: 47). Like the initial restructuring postulated by Halliday the account is both unclear in that it fails to specify a developmental process and nominalistic in that "functional derestriction" is explained by "recasting" the concept of function.

2.1.5 *Prerequisites for explaining language development*

An issue of particular importance in evaluating the studies reviewed above is the status of the features they incorporate in their explanations of language development. All of the studies attempt to explain how it is that the child comes to master the system of language. Thus, a general requirement of the different models is that they be models of the child's system; that they describe the child's development in terms of concepts and strategies that the child might legitimately bring to bear on his or her mastery of speech and that the role of such concepts and strategies be open to potential investigation. This could be termed the problem of the psychological reality of explanations.

This question can be approached at two levels: the description of the language system itself, and the implication of other psychological processes in the development of the language system.

As far as the language system is concerned many of the accounts are clearly deficient. Greenfield and Smith's claim that aspects of the situation are an element of the child's message makes an incoherent claim about how the child might use an aspect of the situation as a structural element of his or her message. Bloom's division of utterances into substance and function words is essentially a categorization derived from adult grammar, as is Nelson's more elaborate system. Grammatical categories, however disguised, have no psychological reality in the language of a child that lacks a grammar. In contrast, the systems of categorization adopted by Dore and Halliday are a deliberate attempt to take account of the functions that language serves for the child.

The picture reverses somewhat when the processes that are implicated in the development of language are considered. Neither Dore nor Halliday specify plausible developmental processes that might account for changes in the child's system. The accounts of Bates *et al.*, Bloom, Greenfield and Smith, and Nelson all argue that language development is related to, and directly depends upon, more general processes of cognitive change. These arguments at least allow further investigation of the hypothesized relations. The accounts differ somewhat in the relations they see between cognitive and linguistic factors. Greenfield and Smith see a fairly direct link between cognitive structures and language structures. Bloom, on the other hand, regards the derivation of semantic concepts of agent, action, etc. as a step towards learning specific related syntactic structures. Nelson and Bates *et al.* are more neutral as to what level of linguistic description is ultimately necessary.

One common feature of all the accounts is an emphasis on naming and, in some cases, an attempt to explain the concept of naming. All of the studies emphasize that the development of naming is the immediate precursor to the development of structured utterances. However, none of the accounts offers an adequate explanation of the development of naming. Both Bates *et al.* and Bloom relate naming to Stage VI of sensorimotor development; Bates *et al.* see a relation between the development of naming and the development of symbolic behaviour, while Bloom relates naming to the final stage of the development of object permanence. Neither appeal has sufficient justification for the issue to be left at that. The following sections contain a more detailed examination of the development of naming.

2.2 The development of reference

The issues of reference are central issues which any theory of language development has to contend with. Among the different problems that must be tackled are the following: (a) how does a child come to learn the concept that names denote objects, (b) how does a child learn what class of objects a name denotes, (c) what is the course of development of pronominalization and anaphora? The first of these issues is of central concern here. The second is of concern in so far as it could be contended that an account of the development of the intensional criteria for class membership might also constitute an account of the development of the concept of naming. The development of referential skills of pronominalization and anaphora, although a necessary part of a complete treatment of the development of reference, will not be pursued here (cf. Bloom, Lightbown & Hood, 1975; Nelson, 1975).

2.2.1 *Ostensive definitions*

Some accounts of naming (e.g. Quine, 1960) argue that names are learnt as a result of a series of ostensive definitions by the adults with whom a child interacts. An objection against such an account is that the method of ostensive definition is inherently ambiguous; for the procedure to work the child must initially know what aspect of the designated object he or she is supposed to attend to: whether the object itself or one of its various properties or component parts. This difficulty has been pointed out by Wittgenstein (1953). Harrison (1972), however, regards this argument against ostensive definitions as inconclusive. He argues as follows: Wittgenstein's account only demonstrates that logically there is a possibility of error in ostensive definition. But this merely shows that the procedure is not foolproof; the logical possibility of error does not mean that, in practice, the ambiguity inherent in the procedure could not be overcome. However, Harrison continues, while ostensive definition might work in practice with a child already in possession of the concept of naming it is incapable of explaining the origin of the concept itself as there is no explanation of why an ostensive definition should be taken as constituting a name by a child ignorant of the concept of naming.

The practice of ostensive definition would thus, at best, address the issue of how a child already in possession of the concept of naming might learn new names. It could not account for the initial acquisition of the concept.

2.2.2 *Class extension and naming*

It might seem that an account of the development of an understanding of the class extension of names would also constitute an account of the development of the concept of naming. Although this thesis has rarely been specifically defended it is tacitly present in a number of accounts of language development. A recent example is Clark (1973). The central question to which Clark addresses herself is this: how are words used to refer to or represent external objects and events appropriately? In answering this question it is the conditions of appropriateness that are of concern to Clark; the concept of representation is taken for granted. Clark argues that a child "attaches meaning to a word" on the basis of some perceptual feature of an object which a word has been used to name. As an example, suppose a child learns the word 'dog'. He or she might use one feature, say being four-legged, to represent the meaning of 'dog' and so the set of objects for which *dog* is used might include a variety of other four-legged animals such as cows, sheep or cats. With the addition of other features besides being four-legged to the meaning of 'dog' the child will gradually narrow down the meaning of 'dog' until its meaning coincides with the adult meaning of 'dog'.

The notion of "feature" is crucial to Clark's account. The idea that the meaning of a word is given by a set of primitive semantic features is not a new one (see Nelson, 1974). Features, in Clark's view, are derived from percepts. This, however, is of little help in explaining the origin of features, as the concept of a percept is at least as vague as the concept of a feature. In support of her view that words are used to refer to some set of features rather than to whole objects Clark argues that "there is no a priori reason for the child to respect either adult or biological taxonomies when he first begins to learn the meaning of a word" (1973: 74–5). But this can hardly be a sufficient justification for opting for a feature-based theory. There may be reasons, whether or not they are *a priori* ones, for taxonomies to be respected, as Rosch and her associates have recently suggested (Rosch, Mervis, Gray, Johnson & Boyes-Braem, 1976). A plausible case for a feature-theory must rest on more positive arguments than this. The central weakness of Clark's account as an explanation of the concept of naming is that the processes of representation and "attaching meaning to a word" are the starting-points of her investigation. There is no account given of how a child learns that language can represent the world (among its other functions). At best, Clark's account is aimed at the second of the problems earlier identified: the problem of class extension.

Is feature-theory then an adequate solution to the problem of class extension? Children do sometimes overextend the meaning of a name by using the name to refer to a wider class of objects than conventional usage dictates. This evidence is consistent with the theory. But children do not always overextend the meaning of words. In such cases feature-theory seems to be driven to the conclusion that a child has either happily picked out some combination of features that gives, more or less, the correct meaning of that word or has picked out a set of features that restricts the application of the word to a more limited class than usual. This reveals a central weakness of feature-theory, at least as applied to the learning of names: when there are overextensions the theory works; when there are not it does not fail.

2.2.3 *Holophrases*

It has sometimes been claimed that children's speech during the one-word stage is holophrastic. Ingram (1974) has distinguished two different types of claim that can be made when the notion of a holophrase is invoked. The first claim is that one-word utterances must be regarded as full utterances if the child's behaviour is to be properly understood. Thus Stevenson (1893: 120) remarks:

When a very young child says "water", he is not using the word merely as the name of the object so designated by us, but with the value of an assertion something like, "I want water" or "there is water", the distinction of meaning between the two expressions being shown by the child's tone of utterance.

This view of holophrases emphasizes the fact that utterances must be viewed in terms of the communicative intention of the speaker. The second view is that one-word utterances should be treated as representations of entire sentences (McNeill, 1970). On this view one-word utterances are derived from a deep structure sentence, but only one element of the deep structure is realized in the surface structure. Ingram (1974: 4) remarks:

In the example of the child who says "water" to mean "I want water", this approach would state that "water" has the grammatical role of Object, and that the other two categories have been deleted, due to some restriction on the length of the utterance.

That particular claim carries little conviction; the arguments against invoking deletion rules to explain one-word utterances have already been presented. However, a more neutral, and more vague, claim has also been made (Bruner, 1975a: 271) about holophrases, that proposes a radical solution to the issue of naming: it denies that naming is an issue.

It seems highly unlikely that naming is what in fact is at issue. For as I have argued in a previous paper (1975b), and as Bloom (1973), Greenfield and Smith (1976) and others, I think, abundantly illustrated, the child's holophrases are grammatically contextualized in a Fillmore-like (1968) case form that highlights some aspect of who is doing what with what object toward whom in whose possession and in what location and often by what instrumentality.

This claim, however, fails to dissolve the issue of naming, as it overstates the case for holophrases and the evidence in their favour. Even if it is true that names are sometimes used in reference to "some aspect of who is doing what with what object toward whom in whose possession and in what location" it is not necessarily true that names are always a reference to such events. In fact the evidence points to the fact that this use of names develops some time after conventional naming. Greenfield and Smith (1976) found that naming occurred before holophrastic uses of names. Ingram (1971, 1974), surveying Leopold's diary (1939–49), reports that the first use of names by Hildegard (Leopold's daughter) was to name objects, with holophrastic use only subsequently developing. Bloom (1973) and Halliday (1975) also report the prominence of naming in their studies and Clark's (1973) review of diary studies indicates a similar result. Holophrases, in the grammatical interpretation of that term, seem to follow rather than precede or displace the development of naming. How they ought to be explained is, of course, a moot point.

2.2.4 *Naming as a conceptual development*

A common problem in the acquisition of any structure, be it biological, behavioural, or conceptual, is the following: the end-product of development is commonly derived from more primitive structures by a series of transformations of some sort during which the product in development undergoes internal reorganization. To understand the course of development in such cases one has to understand the processes of transformation. Piaget's (1937) theory of the development of the object-concept, and subsequent work based on that theory (cf. Bower, 1974; Gratch, 1975; Harris, 1975) is a classic psychological example.

Does the concept that objects have names develop from more primitive origins by a series of structural transformations of the concept itself? Nelson (1974) has presented such a case. Nelson argues that whole objects take on definition as concepts in virtue of their functional or dynamic relations. A concept consists initially of an individual element unseparated from its functional relations (relations such as: moves, makes a noise, etc.). As the object is encountered in a variety of different situations some relations will be found to be consistent across most situations. A ball, for example, will roll and bounce. These consistent relations become the functional core of the concept. Other relations may be seen as irrelevant and these will cease to be part of the concept. Given a functional concept a child can identify new instances of the concept if the relationships of a new instance are identical to an already existing functional core. Where several different exemplars of a concept are encountered, a child may notice that common attributes are shared by each exemplar and may rely on these attributes to recognize new instances of the concept outside the context of its core actions and relationships. At this point the concept contains functional–relational information as well as perceptual–descriptive information. At any point in the stage of concept formation a name may be attached to the concept, although the existence of concepts need not lead directly to naming them. "Naming may begin", Nelson remarks (1974: 279), "when the child recognizes that a word used by others is used consistently in the context of instances of one of his concepts."

Thus, names are attached initially to some of the child's functional concepts. Nelson's (1973) earlier finding that the initial names a child learns refer to objects that have "salient properties of change" is consistent with her view of the relationship between concepts and names.

The next stage of Nelson's account must be to explain how conceptual differentiation further occurs to allow naming independently of the functional relationships into which objects enter. She suggests that an initial concept contains two potentially separable sorts of functions: those that are relatively specific to particular objects (e.g. balls roll and bounce) and those that are relatively general across a large variety of objects (concepts of agency, action, etc.). She suggests that specific and general relationships in a concept are differentiated so that (a) object-specific relations alone form part of the object concept and (b) general relations that are common across many different object concepts achieve the status of concepts in their own right. According to Nelson these developments lead to, respectively, the development of naming and the development of language structure.

When the differentiation of the functional core from other relational specifications has taken place, the child becomes able both to name the concept independently of its involvement in a defining relationship (for example, as represented in a picture or in a new location) and to express the concept and the relations independently, thereby making it possible to form relational statements, that is, two-word (or longer) utterances.

(1974: 280)

Nelson's model is the only existing model that attempts to trace the emergence of the concept of naming. It must be recognized that at present the model is entirely theoretical. Nelson specifies a process of conceptual differentiation that could take place and that could explain both the development of naming and the development of language structure. But there is little empirical evidence that the process of concept formation is as described. That may merely reflect a lag between theory and evidence. But what sort of evidence? We can never observe concepts directly, we can only make inferences on the basis of behavioural evidence. I have earlier appealed to the principle that we should attribute to any organism the minimum degree of conceptual organization that is neccessary to account for its behaviour. It is not obvious, to me at any rate, to what extent Nelson's model admits of behavioural evidence. The difficulty is that the complexity of the concept's specification is much greater than the complexity of the organism's behaviour. It is unclear what could constitute sufficient evidence for the sorts of concepts that Nelson proposes.

Putting that difficulty aside, what of the major thesis – that of conceptual differentiation? How do theory and evidence relate here? The major behavioural advance that must be accounted for is the development of naming proper, and the subsequent development of structured speech. Nelson argues as follows:

> Many researchers...have noted that children very frequently show a marked acceleration of labeling objects and learning names for new objects just prior to producing two-word sentences (e.g., Halliday, 1975; Nelson, 1973). Such a correlation is implied by the course of development sketched here, in that labeling and combining are both manifestations of an emerging ability to detach the concept from its original relationships and put it into relation with independently defined concepts.
>
> (1974: 282)

But if the correlation is implied the implication is weak indeed. Nelson's model is a model of how particular concepts develop. It is assumed (reasonably) that there will be relations between different concepts thus allowing the differentiation of object-specific relations and general relations. That leads to a network of concepts adequate to the observed semantic relations of initial word combinations. But there is nothing in this that implies a marked acceleration of labelling objects or a *subsequent* development of structured utterances. The claim that there is is merely a gratuitous accommodation of the model to known facts. And indeed this weakness characterizes the whole model; it has no particular behavioural implications. The theory might seem to predict that initially objects will only be named when perceived in some functional relation. But suppose we observe a case where no functional relation is evident. That would not be a counterexample, for names may be attached to concepts at any point in the concept's development and all we need do is specify a more advanced concept to get over that little difficulty. As Nelson does not specify any behavioural criteria for inferring concepts there are no constraints on how advanced conceptual differentiation may be when any particular word is observed in use.

2.2.5 *Joint attention and naming*

One of the principal general arguments concerning language development in recent years is that particular communicative acts do not arise *de novo* but develop from more primitive means of preverbal communication. We have seen (2.1.3) how this argument was applied to the development of requests by Bates *et al.* (1975) and also to the development of declaratives, although the latter argument was found not to carry conviction. It seems obvious that there is no direct sense in which naming could be carried out without the use of words and that at least distinguishes naming from pragmatic speech-acts such as requesting. Nevertheless, it has been argued that there are other, less direct, preverbal developments that contribute to the development of naming. An understanding of these developments would help us appreciate what type of achievement naming is for the child.

There are many ways of referring to any object; an object can have many names. As Brown (1958) has pointed out one object could be called *dime, coin, money, change, it, that, thing,* and so on. In the face of such a proliferation of possible referring expressions for any object a number of writers (Harrison, 1972; Olson, 1970; Rommetveit, 1974) have been concerned to point out that the expression chosen is one that serves to identify the referent in question from competing alternatives. The central point of such accounts of reference is that the relation between a referring expression and a referent is not one of simply attaching an inevitable name or a description to an object but of choosing an expression that is both intersubjectively and contextually unambiguous. To draw the listener's attention to a particular object, the speaker must choose an expression that allows the listener to distinguish the referent from other relevant objects. A prerequisite of success is the joint attention of listener and speaker to the same situation. The development of joint attention in mother–infant dyads has therefore been seen as an important preverbal step in the development of reference by Bruner (1975a, 1975b). Bruner's contention is that the development of joint attention creates an intersubjective framework where there is implicit social agreement about an activity, attending, that is a necessary part of reference. Bruner further argues that the topic–comment structure of language reflects the processes of attention. Following Neisser (1967) he regards the process of attention as one of analysis-by-synthesis:

a process of positing wholes (topics) to which parts or features or properties may be related and from which the new wholes may be constructed. The predicational rules of natural language are surely a well-adapted vehicle for expressing the results of such attentional processing: topic–comment structure in language permits an easy passage from feature to its context and back, while topicalization provides a ready means for regrouping new sets of features into hypothesized wholes to be used as topics on which to comment. (Bruner, 1975b: 4–5)

Let us first consider how joint attention develops and then its relevance to the development of reference. Studies of the development of joint attention have revealed that visual co-orientation is initially due largely to the efforts of the mother. Collis and Schaffer (1975) and Collis (1977) have shown that with infants of 10 months mothers allow their attention to be directed by the infants' behaviour and continually monitor the infants' focus of visual attention. However, there was no evidence that infants tended to follow the mothers' direction of gaze more often than would be expected by chance (Collis, 1977). This finding conflicts with the results reported by Scaife and Bruner (1975) where there was a clear tendency for infants from 8 months old to follow another's direction of gaze. The differences may be due to differences in experimental technique. In Scaife and Bruner's experiment an experimenter established eye contact with an infant and then looked to one side, either right or left. In the Collis and Schaffer (1975) and Collis (1977) experiments mother and infant were engaged in unrestrained interaction in a laboratory. Mutual gaze did not necessarily precede a line of gaze in this situation. These experiments seem to show that from 8 months onwards infants are capable of following the line of gaze of another person provided eye contact is first established. In the absence of initial eye contact infants do not appear to consistently follow another's gaze at this age.

Other studies of joint attention have focused on the use of pointing in mother–infant dyads. Murphy and Messer (1977) found that by the time infants were 9 months old mothers used the pointing gesture to attract the infants' attention. When these 9-month-old infants were compared with 14-month-old infants it was found that the mothers of the 9-month-old group often supplemented their pointing gesture with additional cues. The abilities of the two groups of infants to follow a point differed. The 9-month-old infants were best at following a point where the relevant object was in the same visual field as the pointing hand. Most infants of this age failed to follow a point across their midline (i.e. where the infant would have to turn through 90 degrees, having observed the pointing hand, in order to locate the object). Infants of 14 months had no difficulty in following either type of point and many of these infants were also observed to point themselves. Collis and Schaffer (1975) noted that mothers not only looked at the same toy as the infant but often went on to label it verbally and comment on it. However, they did not present any systematic data on this point. Collis (1977) did present data on the incidence of naming by mothers. He found that when a mother named a toy the infant was much more likely to be looking at the toy that was being identified than at any other toy, but the number of occurrences of naming was also small. On the other hand Murphy and Messer (1977) reported that only 5 out of 428 points were unaccompanied by maternal vocalizations and over 40 per cent of these vocalizations consisted of naming. However, these studies may not tell us very much about the relation between joint attention and naming outside the laboratory, for it must be rare for a mother and an infant to sit down and be confronted, as they were in these studies, by a carefully arranged array of novel toys.

Studies by Murphy (1978) and Ninio and Bruner (1978) add the desired element of realism. Both studies report data from sequences of picture-book reading, an activity that mothers and infants commonly engage in. Murphy's is a laboratory study in which the mother was asked to look at the book with her infant and the subsequent behaviour was recorded. Mothers with infants of 9, 14, 20 and 24 months old were compared. Ninio and Bruner report a longitudinal study of one mother–infant dyad between the ages of 8 and 18 months. The data in this study are naturalistic in that book reading was spontaneously engaged in by the mother–infant dyad.

Naming, by the mother, is not a random affair. In Ninio and Bruner's study 76 per cent of all observed naming by the mother occurred in picture-book sequences. Within these sequences several other regularities were apparent. The mother's utterances were remarkably consistent over the period studied. They consisted of four key utterance-types: a call for attention from the infant, e.g.

look; a query to the infant, e.g. *what's that?*; a name, e.g. *it's a dog*, and feedback to a response from the infant, e.g. *yes*. Some, or all, of this sequence of utterances was regularly observed. Murphy also found that for all age-groups in her study a call for attention (*look/see*) was a frequent accompaniment of naming and pointing by the mother.

How did the infants' participation develop? At the beginning of Ninio and Bruner's study the infant was 8 months old and his participation in the dialogue while looking at picture-books was minimal by adult standards. However, in common with Snow's (1977a) findings, Ninio and Bruner report that the interaction was structured by the mother as a well-regulated conversation with any minimal participation by the infant accepted as a turn in the conversation. Initially the mother accepted her infant's vocalizations as attempts at labelling, and confirmed his attempts by supplying the correct label. But, when instances of naming by the infant began at 14 months, other vocalizations were now challenged with a *what's that?* query, where previously they had been accepted and unchallenged. When the infant at this age pointed to an object the mother still tended to name the object for the infant. Murphy's study reports similar results for infant pointing and maternal naming at 14 months. By 20 months things are different: the child tended to both point and name, and when it was the mother who pointed she was likely to ask the child to name the object pointed at (in contrast to the behaviour of mothers of 14-month-old infants who were likely to provide the name themselves).

Is joint attention the preverbal behaviour from which naming develops? I believe it is, provided that the joint attention occurs in the context of a ritual naming game. In the next section I will elaborate on this. I began this section by pointing out that a thing can have many names. This fact has sometimes been used to dispute the importance of naming (cf. Bruner, 1975a; Olson, 1970). If the point is that things do not have *a* name then that point is well-taken and an adequate theory of reference must specify how the relations between the different possible names any object may have actually develop. But that should not obscure the point, as it sometimes does, that the concept that things can be named still requires a developmental explanation. I now turn to that explanation.

2.2.6 *A theory of naming*

Looking at picture-books maximizes joint attention and it also appears to maximize naming by the mother, as Ninio and Bruner (1978) have shown. Do children therefore learn the names of objects because they repeatedly hear the same objects named while looking at picture-books?[3] Before answering that question, let us reconsider the words 'name' and 'naming'. In the situations described above I have regarded any word we would recognize as a noun in the adult language as a name, whether it was used by the child or the mother, and I have regarded instances of the use of the word as instances of naming. I have no doubt that this is an accurate characterization of the mother's behaviour, but it is not necessarily an accurate characterization of the child's behaviour because nothing has been done to show that the child possesses the concept that words name objects. I would suggest that the child does not possess the concept of naming when he or she first learns to pair words with objects in rituals such as story-book reading. My further suggestion is that the words the child initially learns in these situations are learnt as a means of participating in a ritual activity that concerns talking about objects. The child first learns the words and later learns that these words are names. The key element in learning that words are names is an insight by the child that *the behaviour previously engaged in* in ritual situations (such as picture-book reading) can be taken to constitute a special type of language-use: naming.

The appeal to the concept of insight is quite deliberate. Insight is a psychological process of common experience (though much ignored theoretically, with a few exceptions, notably Kohler, 1925). The basic achievement of an insight is a relatively sudden realization of some previously unseen structural relationship. While

---

[3] Ninio and Bruner (1978: 5) point out that pictures have the further interesting characteristics: "pictures, being two-dimensional representations of three-dimensional objects, have special visual properties: they can be perceived both as a two-dimensional object AND as representing a three-dimensional visual scene. This poses a conflict for a child, one which he solves increasingly by assigning privileged, autonomous status to pictures as visual objects. There is steadily less evidence of the child trying to manipulate, grasp or scratch pictured objects on a page. This process might be one of the stepping stones to grasping arbitrary symbolic representation in language, since visual representations are themselves arbitrary in the sense that a crucial object property, i.e. graspability, is missing."

the environment can supply the child with names for objects and a context appropriate to the learning of these names it cannot supply the concept of naming. This the child must construct out of his or her own experience in the environment. We know very little about that construction process; indeed it has been frequently ignored in accounts of the development of naming. However, the product of the child's attempts to construct an understanding of the relation between words and objects I suggest to be a relatively sudden realization that the words are names for the objects. On the antecedent side the appeal to insight is motivated by the fact that the ritual nature of many naming games will be such that the child's use of names will have the characteristics and context appropriate to naming even if the activity is not conceptualized by the child as one of naming. (And even if the child learns to utter very few words in these situations the role of his or her comprehension of the mother's utterances must not be ignored.) The fact that children's initial use of names has often been regarded as referentially idiosyncratic (Bloom, 1973; Leopold, 1939–49; Piaget, 1945; Vygotsky, 1934; Werner & Kaplan, 1963) lends support to the view that the concept of naming does not precede the use of names. On the consequent side the appeal to insight is motivated by the sudden increase in naming that is frequently observed towards the middle of the second year (Halliday, 1975; Leopold, 1939–49; Nelson, 1973). Many of the names learnt during this period are the names of objects that are of no functional significance to the child. The child acts as if he or she had discovered that things have names by seeking to discover the names of objects encountered.

This account of naming raises a number of further issues. The first concerns the generality of the hypothesis. Not all children are observed to increase their vocabularies rapidly, and undoubtedly not all children receive environmental support in the form of ritual naming games. The two facts may be related. The achievement of the concept of naming, I have suggested, crucially depends on the nature of the child's previous experience and one of the consequences of the attainment of the concept is a sudden increase in the vocabulary of names. But language is not only about naming, however crucial naming may be, and a child who does not learn many names will nevertheless learn to talk. If there are referential and expressive speakers, as Nelson (1973) has suggested, then the referential speakers may be the children who have played ritual naming games and the expressive speakers those who have not. That, at least, is what the present account predicts. This is not to say that expressive speakers learn to talk by bypassing the concept of naming but rather than the achievement of that concept will be slower and its manifestation less dramatic than in referential speakers.

A second issue concerns the development of grammatical structure. Rapid increases in naming are usually quickly followed by the emergence of two-word utterances (Halliday, 1975; Leopold, 1939–49; Nelson, 1973). There is little difficulty in accounting for this. If objects have names to represent them then, by generalization, so should actions, attributes, and so on. And as objects act, or are acted upon, then the child's description of these events will necessarily need to encode the different aspects of the event for which he or she has separate words. It is central to this account that the development of names for objects precedes the development of both structured speech and the development of words that describe actions and attributes. These issues will be considered in Chapter 5.

The account of naming offered above has concentrated its emphasis on the ritual interactions that may help a child to conceptualize the relationship between a name and an object. It is commonly held that the ability to conceptualize this relationship is dependent on the symbolic capacity that characterizes Stage VI of Piaget's theory of sensorimotor development. If this argument is valid then the conceptualization that I have characterized as insight may itself depend on more general processes of cognitive development. The following section examines this possibility.

2.2.6 *Words and symbols*

In *La formation du symbole chez l'enfant* (rendered into English as *Play, dreams and imitation in childhood*) Piaget attempts to trace the emergence of symbolic behaviour, including language, from its origins in sensorimotor development. Piaget argues that language only becomes possible with the development of thought in general and of the ability to represent the world by means of symbols in particular. This development is the end-point of sensorimotor development. Piaget's view is that all knowledge originates with action; during sensorimotor development the child's schemes are schemes for acting on the world and their general form is not mentally represented independently of particular applications of the scheme. Throughout sensorimotor development there is a gradual dissociation of general form from particular content. The achievement of sensorimotor intelligence is to effect a separation of form from content, a separation referred to by Furth (1969) as the "functional interiorization" of schemes. The schemes are mentally represented independently of acts following "functional interiorization".

There are two senses in which Piaget uses the concept of representation. In its broad sense representation is identical with thought and based on a system of mental operations which are the result of the functional interiorization of schemes. A narrower sense of representation concerns the internal image of an event (literally a re-presentation). The internal image is referred to by Piaget as a 'symbol'. It is the development of the ability to represent events, in this latter sense, that Piaget regards as relevant to an understanding of language. Symbols and words are regarded alike by Piaget as manifestations of a symbolic function which he has described as follows:

It consists in the ability to represent something (a signified something: object, event, conceptual scheme, etc.) by means of a "signifier" which is differentiated and which serves only a representative purpose: language, mental image, symbolic gesture, and so on. (Piaget and Inhelder, 1966: 51)

Piaget argues that there is a functional unity between the different forms of representation. They evolve from sensorimotor schemes and in all cases the criterion for inferring a representational element is "the deferred character of the reaction" (Piaget, 1945: 98). In the case of language Piaget proceeds as follows: words do not initially represent objects; the first words a child uses have an intermediate status between sensorimotor schemes and representational elements: "[The] first verbal schemas are merely sensory-motor schemas in process of becoming concepts; they are neither purely sensory-motor schemas nor clear concepts" (1945: 219). This rather baffling claim is related to Piaget's contention that the capacity for constructing conceptual representation is not present till the end of the sensorimotor period. Prior to this, concepts are referred to as 'preconcepts', and language has a likewise inter-mediate status between schemes and concepts. Language begins, Piaget argues, with verbal recall of an event. He cites several examples of recall to illustrate

the turning point at which language in process of construction ceases to be merely an accompaniment to an action in progress, and is used for the reconstitution of a past action, thus providing a beginning of represen-tation. The word then begins to function as a sign, that is to say, it is no longer merely a part of the action, but evokes it. Then and then only is the verbal schema detached from the sensory-motor schema and acquires...the function of re-presentation, *i.e.*, of new presentation.

(1945: 222–3)

The claim here advanced by Piaget is that the existence of the representational element is proved by the deferred character of the reaction. However, in his desire to provide a unitary operational criterion for representation Piaget has failed to see that the signifier–signified relationship between word and object is inde-pendent of this criterion as it is neither a logical nor, in the case of language, a methodological necessity that recall be part of any signifier–signified relationship. In language a signifier–signified relationship can be recognized on the grounds advanced by Halliday (1975) among others in the case of naming: the words have no pragmatic or utilitarian purpose; their sole function is to name the object. Halliday also reported that the informative use of language (verbal recall) was the last function to develop and that some structured speech was already evident before verbal recall occurred. This fact is inconsistent with the possibility that verbal recall is the beginning of a signifier–signified relationship in language.

Apart from the unnecessary emphasis on recall as a criterion for inferring a signifier–signified relationship and the difficulties presented by the verbal jungle of Piaget's concepts, there are further reasons for resisting his account of language development.

Piaget's neglect of the communicative functions of language derives from his general neglect of the social construction of knowledge. His theory of development is primarily a theory of the development of knowledge of the world of physical objects as a child with rather abstract epistemic interests might conceive it. Although interaction between organism and environment plays a primary role in Piaget's theory of sensorimotor development, he overlooks the fact that, as Newson and Newson (1975: 437) put it: "the object with which the human infant interacts most often, and most effectively, particularly in the earliest stages of development, is almost invariably another human being".

Despite the difficulties which attach to Piaget's own account, a number of writers have turned to it for an explanation of the process of language development in general, and naming in particular. Some do little more than reiterate his account with minor modifications. Sinclair (1970) regards words as "translations" of sensorimotor schemes. Neither this nor her subsequent (1971, 1973) articles clarify how words are "translated". McNeill (1975) argues that sensorimotor schemes provide the basic organizational structure from which speech derives. To this claim (the cognition hypothesis) McNeill adds that higher level conceptual processes "take over" the organization of speech schemes from sensorimotor schemes as the child develops. These higher level processes (called 'syntagmas' by McNeill, after Kozhevnikov & Chistovich, 1965) "emerge" with the development of the symbolic function. Morehead and Morehead (1974) likewise reiterate Piaget's claims. Bates (1976), like Bates *et al.* (1975), presents a model that relates language-use to Piagetian stages. She also appeals to the development of a symbolic function to explain how words come to represent objects and reiterates Piaget's claim that it is imitation and play that establish the symbolic function. When this function has been established the child becomes able to represent mentally any of his or her existing schemes. Thus, words come to represent mentally the scheme to which they originally belonged.

Despite the repeated faith in the power of a symbolic function none of the accounts explains how it is that a symbolic function facilitates language development. All of the accounts accept that words come to be symbols and then invoke a symbolic function to explain this development. While the accounts avoid circularity by explaining the development of a symbolic function in terms of imitation and play (although arguably this only pushes circularity one step further back) they sacrifice clarity by invoking an ill-understood process to explain, *deus ex machina*, how words become signifiers.[4] It is possible that as the processes of specific symbolic functions are explored in more detail the need to postulate a ubiquitous general process will disappear. At any rate a more detailed investigation of the development of symbolic behaviour, including naming, will need to be carried out before the precise role of a symbolic function in development is determined.

2.3 Summary

The principal psychological processes implicated in language development focus, respectively, on the contingencies of communicative interaction between mother and child and on the cognitive structures that may underlie the child's observed use of language. Those who regard communicative interaction as the key to language development emphasize that language is a mode of human activity and that the child is gradually initiated into the variety of forms of social intercourse and relationships that involve the use of language. While this approach gives a plausible account of the development of pragmatic uses of language, such as requests, it is less obvious how it might account for the development of referential uses of language. The particular problem with reference is explaining the conceptual achievement of a word–referent relationship. Various approaches to the problem of reference were discussed. Theories that emphasize conceptual differentiation (Nelson, 1974; Piaget, 1945) were found to lack an adequate grounding in clear behavioural evidence for the processes they implicate. Apart from this there is the prevalent tacit assumption that the child constructs a concept of reference as a result of casual

---

[4] Piaget's (1945) concern was to discuss the operation of what he identified as a "symbolic function". Most of his book deals with a period when this function is already present and relatively little consideration is given to the issue of how symbols develop. This is true even of play and imitation, which he *identifies* as having symbolic content at Stage VI of sensorimotor development. On the basis of this identification he postulates the existence of a symbolic function.

encounters with the language of others. Against this it was argued that there are specific types of ritual interaction between caretakers and children that may greatly facilitate the development of the concept of a referential relationship between word and object. Such encounters allow the child to learn to use names. The realization of what that use conceptually entails follows later for the child. Insight was hypothesized to be the psychological process by which the concept of naming is eventually arrived at.

3

The development of conversation

3.0 Doing talking

Utterances must be both meaningful and appropriate to the situation if ordinary communication is to be successful. The appropriateness or inappropriateness of an utterance is not revealed by analysis of its grammatical structure. A complete account of linguistic communication cannot ignore the variables that determine why one utterance rather than another is spoken or why a particular utterance may be judged appropriate in one context but not in another. Conversational analysis is concerned with how participants structure the social task of talking.

Until comparatively recently the question of how children learn the wide variety of skills necessary to the competent communicant has been relatively neglected in studies of language development. Historically this neglect might be accounted for, in part, by the predominant emphasis on questions of linguistic structure in children's speech and by the attendant assumption that psycholinguistic competence is sufficient for communicative competence. That assumption is no longer in the least tenable (Campbell & Wales, 1970; Glucksberg, Krauss, & Higgins, 1975; Hymes, 1971). To be a successful communicant a child must eventually learn how to talk, what to say, and when to say it. It has been argued that the origins of conversation can be traced to the earliest social interactions between mothers and infants (Freedle & Lewis, 1977; Lewis & Freedle, 1973). A "conversation-like" organization has been reported in infant feeding (Kaye, 1977), in mother–infant eye contact (Brazelton, Koslowski, & Main, 1974; Fogel, 1977; Jaffe, Stern, & Peery, 1973; Stern, 1974; Stern, Beebe, Jaffe, & Bennett, 1977), and in the vocal interaction between mother and infant (Bateson, 1971; Snow, 1977a; Trevarthen, 1977). To interpret such claims we must first consider conversational organization.

3.1 The organization of conversation

Literature relevant to the organization of conversation includes
accounts of general principles of conversation (Grice, 1975, 1978;
Sacks, Schegloff, & Jefferson, 1974); detailed studies of particular
sequences of conversation, such as openings and closings (Schegloff,
1968; Schegloff & Sacks, 1973); and studies of the non-verbal
management of conversational interaction (Argyle & Cook, 1976;
Beattie, 1978b; Duncan, 1972; Duncan & Fiske, 1977; Ekman &
Friesen, 1969). Grice (1975) points out that conversation is
characteristically a cooperative effort between the participants and,
on this assumption, Grice has formulated a series of maxims that
speakers will follow if they are intent on conversing. Speakers will,
in general, make their contribution as informative as is necessary,
speak the truth, make their contribution relevant, and avoid
obscurity of expression, ambiguity and prolixity. Grice was not
concerned to demonstrate that speakers always follow these maxims
but to point out that following them entailed the implication of
various things that were unsaid. That issue will not be pursued here
(see Sadock, 1978; Walker, 1975). The general principle that
conversation is a cooperative activity between two or more participants is a convenient starting-point and leads immediately to the
question of how cooperation is achieved.

Probably the most obvious aspect of the cooperative nature of
conversation is its organization by turns: one party speaks at a time
and there are periodic exchanges of role between the speaker and
(one of) the listener(s). Sacks *et al.* (1974) have attempted to
characterize the organization of turntaking in conversational interaction. Their model of turn-taking has two component parts: a
turn-constructional component and a turn-allocation component.

Turn-constructional component. The basic factors to be considered
here are those relevant to the organization of speech within a
speaking turn. A speaking turn can be considered as the speech of
one participant until either another participant claims a turn, or
the current speaker ends his or her turn with a recognizable
turn-yielding cue (Duncan, 1972). In general the two criteria are
mutually applicable; it is usually the case that one person speaks
at a time, that transitions are smoothly organized, and that

transitions occur at discrete and identifiable points within a conversation. There is a variety of ways in which a conversation can begin and how it does so will depend upon the participants and the nature of the interaction. Unless the participants are already engaged in interaction a conversation is usually initiated through a set of procedures that constitute an agreement to talk. Typical initiation rituals include the following, either alone or in some combination: mutual greeting where the participants are known to each other; self-identification where the participants are not known to each other together with an expressed reason for initiating the conversation; a request to converse. (For the initiation of telephone conversations see Schegloff, 1968.) When the content of the conversation has been introduced it is often the case, particularly for turns of more than minimum length (i.e. those turns that add information as opposed to turns such as short questions that are exclusively concerned with further turn-allocation), that the speaking turn has a three part structure: the first part relates what the speaker says to some preceding utterance(s); the second part is concerned with what the speaker wishes to add; and the third part passes the conversation on to another person (Sacks *et al.*, 1974). Within this framework a further set of requirements operate. Certain forms of address may be more appropriate than others; this will depend on the role and the status relationship between speaker and hearer (Brown & Gilman, 1960; Cicourel, 1972). The assumptions the speaker makes concerning the amount of knowledge the hearer has about the topic under discussion will also influence the form of the message (Garfinkel, 1972; Rommetveit, 1974). Thus, the "same" message may be elaborate or condensed and referents may be identified by technical, non-technical, or metaphoric terms depending on the speaker's audience.

During the course of a speaker's turn listeners do not remain mute and motionless. Listeners engage in a variety of behaviours, both verbal and nonverbal, which contribute an essential part to the conversational interaction. On the nonverbal side these behaviours include nodding, shaking the head, and various facial gestures that serve to indicate the listener's response to the information conveyed. On the verbal side listeners make a variety of utterances such as *uh-uh*, *I see*, *oh no!* and so on that are not generally regarded as constituting separate speaking turns because such utterances do not constitute any further claim to a speaking turn. These utterances have been dubbed "listener responses" by Dittmann and Llewellyn (1968) and "back-channel communication" by Yngve (1970). However, the issue is not entirely without complication. Duncan (1972) regards the following as additional back-channel signals: sentence completion, in which a second participant completes an utterance begun by a first participant; brief requests for clarification; and restatements in a few words of an immediately preceding thought expressed by the previous speaker. It is a moot point whether these latter categories should not be regarded as a speaking turn. In particular, short questions and requests for clarification, unlike the previously described listener responses, serve to indicate that the original speaker's utterance was in some way communicatively incomplete and thus they function as repair techniques in the conversation. If this is so then such utterances deserve separate recognition and analysis rather than assimilation to the category of listener responses, the remainder of which serve a quite separate communicative function.

Turn-allocation component. Turn-allocation may proceed either by speaker selection, in which case the current speaker selects the next speaker, or by self-selection, in which case a new speaker claims a turn on his or her own account (Sacks *et al.*, 1974). A common means of speaker selection is the use of an addressed utterance, frequently an addressed question. An addressed question requires the participant to whom the question is addressed both to take a conversational turn and to produce an utterance that is an appreciable answer to the question asked. Questions can come in a variety of forms: the whole utterance may be planned and uttered as a question or the utterance may be planned and uttered as a statements with a tag question added. Tag questions can be added to the end of any turn as a technique of speaker selection (e.g. *don't you agree?*, *isn't that so?*). Tag questions are not always added directly to the end of a speaking turn; they frequently serve as "post-completers". Post-completers occur when a speaker who has finished a turn, but has failed to allocate the next turn and it has not been claimed by another on his or her completion, then exercises his or her option to continue by adding an utterance such as a tag question thus selecting another as speaker.

If a current speaker ends a turn without selecting the next speaker then self-selection can operate. Speakers use a variety of turn-yielding cues to indicate that they have reached the end of a turn. Duncan (1972) has identified six discrete behavioural cues, which may be displayed either singly or together to indicate the end of a turn. These include intonation, drawl on the final syllable or on the stressed syllable of the clause; various forms of body motion; sociocentric sequences such as *you know*; a drop in pitch or loudness in conjunction with a sociocentric sequence; and the completion of a grammatical clause. A possible addition to these cues is gaze. Kendon (1967) claimed that a "sustained" gaze by the speaker at his interlocutor occurred at the end of a speaking turn but more recent research (Beattie, 1978a; Rutter, Stephenson, Ayling, & White, 1978) has cast some doubt on the generality of this phenomenon. However that issue may be resolved, it is clear that there is a variety of verbal and behavioural cues that serve to indicate the end of a speaking turn. Listeners undoubtedly recognize these cues and their recognition serves to minimize both the gap and the overlap between participants in a conversation.

3.2 The origins of conversation

A number of studies of early mother–infant interaction suggest that the regulation of social behaviour by turn-taking is something that characterizes mother–infant dyads in the earliest months of infancy. Kaye (1977: 89) expresses it as follows:

There is an obvious similarity between the burst–pause pattern in sucking during the first month of human life and later burst–pause cycles of activity. These are found in visual attention to objects (alternating with gaze aversion), face-to-face interaction (cycles of arousal and passivity), trials in skill acquisition, turns in instructional interaction, and language.

What is the obvious similarity between the burst–pause pattern of sucking and turn-taking in conversation? Presumably it is the fact that the behaviour of mother and infant occur in sequence rather than concurrently. But this is almost entirely due to the mother; the mother only acts when the infant has ceased sucking. However, if she does nothing the infant will organize sucking in

essentially the same manner. The only effect the mother's behaviour
has on the infant is to cause a slightly longer delay to the onset
of the next sucking cycle than would be the case if she had not acted
(Kaye, 1977). That there may be some similarity between the
burst–pause pattern of the infant sucking and conversational
turn-taking is, in itself, an unremarkable fact. Is there any causal
relationship? The possibility seems remote. But the fact that the
mother construes the relationship as one involving social reciprocity
may be a clue to the development of turn-taking if we can find
similar patterns of interaction in behaviours that will be later
implicated in conversational exchanges. Even then, much work will
remain to be done, but let us examine the evidence. The two
candidate behaviours are gazing and vocalizing.

3.2.1 *Gazing*

Studies of mother–infant dyads from the sixth week onwards have
revealed that, when mother and infant are engaged in interaction,
the mother typically looks at the infant for relatively long periods
of time by comparison with the average duration of gaze in adult
conversations (Fogel, 1977; Stern, 1974; Stern *et al.*, 1977). A
mother is less likely to look away while the infant is gazing at her
than while the infant is not so gazing (Stern, 1974). During the
periods of the mother's extended gaze the infant's behaviour
consists of cycles of gaze and no-gaze (Brazelton *et al.*, 1974; Fogel,
1977; Stern, 1974). Gaze initiation by the infant tends to occur
when the mother is looking at the infant (not surprising in view
of her periods of extended gaze) and is most likely to occur when
the mother is simultaneously looking, vocalizing, and making face
movements such as smiling and rounding of the mouth (Fogel,
1977; Stern, 1974). Fogel (1977) has reported that the mother
invests more time in these behaviours when the infant is looking
at her; her cycle is systematically expanded during periods of infant
attention and systematically contracted during periods of infant
non-attention. Presumably these expansions are an attempt by the
mother to maintain the infant's attention. There is an obvious
asymmetry in such mother–infant interactions. The mother is
making a considerable effort to establish and maintain a pattern of

communication around the fluctuations in the infant's behaviour (fluctuations which Stern (1974) has suggested may be due to the infant's underlying pattern of biological organization). Kaye (1977) and Fogel (1977) have both used the concept of "framing" to interpret the asymmetry in the mother–infant interaction: the mother is seen as adapting her behaviour to the infant's attention, thus providing a predictable pattern of behaviours that are contingently related to the infant's state. It is suggested that as a result of such framing the infant can gradually achieve intentional control over the activities engaged in. Kaye (1977) has argued that there are three phases in sequences of interaction such as gazing in mother–infant dyads. The first phase is the framing phase. The second phase is one in which there is mutual control of the contingencies, and a sequence may become a goal in itself for both partners as they attempt to initiate it and prolong it. The peekaboo game (Bruner & Sherwood, 1976) is one instance of this. The third phase is one in which one or other partner violates the rule, thus disrupting the sequence. Kaye suggests that rule violation, because it disconfirms the other party's expectations, can serve to confirm the fact that the rule really was what it was thought to be.

The evidence to date seems to point to two consistent findings: that mutual gaze plays a role in adult conversations and that mutual gaze is present in mother–infant interaction. Whether or not there is a causal link between these behaviours remains to be established. In adult conversations the coordination of gazing with vocalizing is of some communicative importance. In mother–infant interaction, although gazing and vocalizing have both been studied, there is little firm evidence on the coordination of gazing with vocalizing for specific communicative purposes. What is obviously lacking at this stage is a developmental history of the role of gaze from its earliest appearance to its integration with vocalizing in intentional communication. Some preliminary data have been presented by Schaffer, Collis, and Parsons (1977). In a comparison of looking and vocalizing in 1- and 2-year-olds they found that 2-year-olds were more likely to look at the mother while they themselves were holding the floor than while the mother was doing so, but that 1-year-olds distributed initiation of looks indiscriminately over both partners' floor-holding episodes. While there is

here a clear developmental difference, it is unclear what its
significance is. Do 2-year-olds behave like adults? It is extremely
difficult to say. The problem is not only the absence of comparative
data but the equivocal nature of the results from studies of gaze
in adult conversations where different patterns of gazing-and-
vocalizing have been found in different contexts (Beattie, 1978a,
b; Kendon, 1967, 1978; Rutter et al., 1978).

Given the present uncertainty about the role of gaze in adult
conversation and the lack of data on developmental changes in
patterns of gazing, any conclusions on the significance of gaze in
mother–infant interactions for conversational organization would
be premature. There remain problems of both a theoretical and
empirical nature. The major theoretical problem on the developmental side is that not enough has been done to show that there
is more than a nominal relation between turn-taking in early social
interaction and turn-taking in conversation. The fact that we may
legitimately speak of turn-taking in early social interaction and
turn-taking in conversation is a fact about the generality of the
concept and the phenomenon, not a demonstration of a causal
relationship between the two types of turn-taking. To make the
point more appreciable consider the opening sentence of Sacks *et
al.* (1974: 696):

Turn-taking is used for the ordering of moves in games, for allocating
political office, for regulating traffic at intersections, for serving customers
at business establishments, and for talking in interviews, meetings,
debates, ceremonies, conversations etc.

The empirical problem follows from this. To show that a behaviour
that occurs in one form in conversational interaction also occurs
in some form in mother–infant interaction does not demonstrate
a developmental relationship from mother–infant interaction to the
organization of conversation. That demonstration requires that the
earlier form of the behaviour be shown to become an organizing
principle of interactions that are more genuinely conversational. To
date there is little evidence on how such behaviours as gaze and
vocalizing co-occur in the course of development, and therefore
little evidence that patterns of gaze in mother–infant interactions
are related to patterns of gaze in conversations.

3.2.2 *Vocalizing*

Conversation is primarily a vocal activity. The study of vocalizing in mother–infant dyads is therefore of considerable interest. It is quite possible that the organization of turn-taking might begin in the early months of life, long before the infant has anything intelligible to say. We might expect such organization to be rudimentary by comparison with adult conversations but a start has to be made somewhere, and if we wish to trace the developmental history of turn-taking, early mother–infant interactions are the most obvious place to begin the search.

Bateson (1971) has reported a study of vocal exchanges in one mother–infant dyad. The infant was 7 weeks old at the beginning of the study and 15 weeks old at the end. Like many other investigators of mother–infant interactions, Bateson makes the point that "the mother's participation is patterned on conversation...her participation is constructed around an expected participation on the infant's part" (1970: 171). In support of this Bateson found that the mean interval between utterance onsets for the mother was significantly longer when the previous utterance was her own utterance than when it was the infant's utterance. In effect, the mother seemed to be allowing the infant time to respond.

If the mother's participation in vocal interchanges is patterned on conversation, is the infant's participation also so patterned? Trevarthen (1977: 249) has described what occurs in a typical mother–infant interaction:

The normal pattern of response by an infant of two months to an attentive, talking mother is as follows – altering of expression and orientation to her face, focalization on her eyes, smiling, increase in body activity, vocalization, often accompanied by a shift of gaze from eyes upwards to the hair, down to the mouth or away from the mother's face to somewhere in the background.

The infant's response when the normal pattern of communication is disrupted is instructive. In a study of 2-month-old infants reported by Trevarthen a partial reflecting mirror was placed between mother and infant. By appropriate arrangement of lighting mother and infant could both see each other. By altering the lighting conditions the mother ceased to see the infant and saw a

projected image of an adult on the mirror. This adult asked the
mother questions by holding up written cards:

The infant, who continued to see the mother, showed strong reactions
of puzzlement and unhappiness when her communication behaviour
switched to adult discourse and became non-contingent with respect to
the infant's actions.
                                                        (1977: 267)

However, when adult behaviour is contingent upon the infant's
action it has a marked effect. Studies using the technique of operant
conditioning have demonstrated that an infant's rate of vocalization
is significantly raised when adults reinforce the infant vocalizations
with a contingent adult vocalization (Rheingold, Gewirtz, & Ross,
1959; Todd & Palmer, 1968; Weisberg, 1963). It thus appears that
infants are sensitive to the way in which adults respond to them
and that their rate of vocalization can be experimentally increased
by contingent reward. However, this merely establishes the fact
that it would be fruitful to look further at dyadic interaction in order
to determine what contingencies actually operate within dyads and
how turn-taking is organized in mother–infant vocal exchanges.

Snow (1977a) has studied the development of conversation
between two mothers and their female infants between 3 and 24
months. Even at 3 months the mothers treated their infants as if
they were partners in an adult-style conversation. At 3 months
behaviours such as smiling, vocalizing, and burping were regarded
as the infant's turn in a conversation. The mothers even refrained
from talking during feeding sessions when the infant had a bottle
in her mouth; in effect refraining from talking when the infant was
prevented from answering. As the infants developed, the pattern
of interaction changed. By 7 months the range of vocalizations to
which the mother would respond had narrowed to "high-quality"
vocalizations (i.e. vocalic or consonantal babble) and some form-
alized imitation games had developed between mother and infant
with rules about the nature of correct response. By 12 months the
infants were responding more reliably to maternal utterances and
were also initiating more of the interactions and by 18 months,
when the children were using words, the mother not only demanded
that the child take her turn but that she provide an appropriate
response. Snow's study suggests that mothers actively induct their

infants into conversational participation by continually updating the demands that are made on the infant. What is of interest in the Snow study is not the nature of the infants' conversational participation at 3 months but that they were treated as conversational partners from this age and that their behaviour was "shaped" by the mother towards conversational participation. This process could not be successful if infants were not responsive to the contingencies that attend their own behaviour.

Surprisingly, there is relatively little information on conversational participation during the time children are initially learning to talk between the ages of 1 and 2 years. A number of diary studies (Halliday, 1975; Leopold, 1939–49; Lewis, 1936) contain incidental remarks on the development of dialogue but little systematic data and, for the most part, documentation is confined to intelligible verbal responses to adult utterances. Halliday (1975: 48–9) reports that at the beginning of the second year his son Nigel was capable of "proto-dialogue" which consisted of responses to calls, greetings, and gifts. In the middle of the second year Nigel learnt (suddenly) to (a) respond to a *wh*-question, (b) respond to a command, (c) respond to a statement, (d) respond to a response, and (e) initiate dialogue by asking the question *what's that?*

However, these achievements only mark the beginning of true dialogue. At the age of 2 there is still little extended dialogue on a particular topic (Bloom, Rocissano & Hood, 1976; Ervin-Tripp & Miller, 1977; Lieven, 1978a, b; and see Keenan & Schieffelin, 1976, on the particular difficulties of maintaining dialogue on a topic). At the age of 2 the ability to use questions as a deliberate conversational strategy has only begun (Smith, 1933; Tyack & Ingram, 1977), and full mastery of the various complexities of questions is not achieved till several years later (Brown, 1968, 1973; Ervin-Tripp & Miller, 1977; Labov & Labov, 1978). The listener responses typical of adult speech are acquired even later (Dittman, 1972), although De Long (1974) has found that children as young as 4 years display kinesic turn-yielding cues. Unfortunately, De Long did not study the effectiveness of these cues in regulating turn-taking.

One feature of conversations between adults and children is the prevalence of questions in the speech adults address to young children (Remick, 1976; Sachs, Brown & Salerno, 1976; Snow, 1972). Questions are a powerful means of turn-allocation, and Snow (1977a) has suggested that this fact accounts for the high frequency of questions in speech to infants. Greenfield and Smith (1976) have argued that questions play a further important role in language development. They regard question–answer dialogue as a means whereby the child learns the syntactic structure of language.

The developmental achievement of dialogue is structural rather than functional: for the first time word is combined with word. In early question–answer dialogue, the child contributes but a single word, but his word is related semantically to the adult's question. Later he, in a sense, internalizes the role of the adult questioner, forming word combinations by himself. Dialogue is thus the two-person model for the child's earliest grammar.   (1976: 209)

Unfortunately, Greenfield and Smith do not support this claim with any evidence that questions and answers relate semantically with any degree of regularity or consistency in adult–child dialogue. Further, the statement that the child "in a sense, internalizes the role of the adult questioner" is, to say the least, obscure and certainly does not seem to constitute an empirically testable claim. While question–answer dialogue may play some part in the child's learning of grammar there is, as yet, no clear evidence that it does so.

   Conversational interaction consists of a good deal more than making verbal utterances. The utterances have to be organized so that they take account of various social conventions and, in addition, the needs of the listener. One of the skills of conversation is the ability to formulate a message in such a way that it takes account of the amount of information necessary to the listener. Adults typically adjust their speech to take account of the presumed competence of their listener (Glucksberg, Krauss & Higgins, 1975). It has long been believed that children lack this ability to adapt their message to the needs of the listener. Piaget (1923) argued that a child's communicative attempts are egocentric, that children are unable to take into account the needs of the listener in communication. Although it is true that a certain amount of a child's communication could be described as egocentric, it seems that the extent to which this is true depends on the nature of the communication. In Piaget's original work children were shown how to work complex (to a child) pieces of equipment such as a water-pump and then asked to describe the working to a second child who had not seen the original demonstration. The children's messages made less than adequate allowance for the needs of the listener. However, it may be that such situations, by their nature, maximize the degree of egocentric speech. More recent experiments have indicated that young children do modify their speech to take account of their listeners' presumed ability to understand. In a study that examined 4-year-old children's explanations of how to work a toy, Shatz and Gelman (1973) compared speech to adults, to other 4-year-olds, and to 2-year-olds. There was no significant difference in the complexity of the speech addressed to adults and to other 4-year-olds, but speech addressed to 2-year-olds was simpler on a variety of measures. However, it is not clear that the ability of 4-year-olds to so adjust their speech is pervasive. Gleason (1973) reported that 4-year-olds typically did not use either a special intonation or repetition, as adults commonly do, in casual talk with 2-year-olds. But, in studies of peer–peer speech of children from $3\frac{1}{2}$ years old De Long (1974), Garvey and Hogan (1973), and Keenan (1974) have found considerable adaptation by the speaker to the verbal and non-verbal behaviour of the listener. It thus appears that egocentrism is a more limited phenomenon than was initially believed. Children do make some attempt to adapt to their listener's needs, but their ability to do so may be constrained by the cognitive complexity of the information they are required to convey.

In conclusion, adults regulate their conversational interactions with young children by altering their speech in predictable ways (see Snow, 1977b; Vorster, 1975 for reviews). One of the effects of the adults' behaviour is the induction of children into the role of conversational partners. But relatively little is known about the children's own conversational abilities. We perhaps no longer regard the characterization of children's communicative abilities as "egocentric" as an accurate or adequate portrayal, but that is a modest conceptual advance that needs to be replaced by a more thorough analysis of how conversational abilities develop.

4

Methodology for a longitudinal study of language development

4.0 Aims and methods of the study

The present study aimed to determine the course of development of communication during the second year of life. The method of study adopted was observation of six children in their own homes in interaction with one of their parents. The families who participated in the study were recruited through mutual friends. The observations commenced as soon as each family had been contacted and had agreed to participate in the study. Observations continued until each child was 2 years old. The children were not selected on any basis of social-class, birth-order, sex, or any other criterion. Four of the children had one older sibling at the commencement of the study. None of these children had a younger sibling. By the time the study was completed one of the first-born children had a younger sibling. All of the families could be broadly regarded as middle-class.

The observations were recorded using a portable video system. Observations were carried out at intervals of approximately one month. Details of the observations are given in Table 1.

Each child was generally observed interacting with his or her mother. Occasionally a child's father was present and interacted with the child during the observation session. These interactions were also recorded. In the case of one child, Brian, caretaking during the period of study was shared by the parents and in this case alternate observations were made of the child interacting with his mother and his father. More frequent observations were made in this case in order to have a reasonable number of sessions where the child interacted with each parent.

The observations were carried out at a time when the child was normally awake and active and the caretaker was free to interact

TABLE 1. *Details of observations*

Child	Age at start of observa-tions (months)	Number of observations	Mean length of an observation (minutes)	Mean interval between observations (days)
Alice	16	8	41	31
Brian	14	14	33	22
Carol	12	12	31	34
David	14	11	31	31
Emily	12	13	30	32
Fiona	12	12	31	34

with the child. The interactions between child and caretaker were not deliberately structured in any way by the observer. Generally the caretaker played with the child during the observation sessions. Occasionally a child involved the observer in a game. On such occasions I willingly participated and resumed filming when the child returned to the caretaker. On a small number of occasions interaction between child and observer was prolonged, and in these cases the caretaker undertook the task of filming the child interacting with the observer until that interaction had ceased. Except for, in some cases, the initial observation session, none of the caretakers was obviously self-conscious in front of the camera. Where possible caretaker and child were included in the picture frame. Where this was not possible the camera followed the child.

4.1 Analysis of the data

The speech of all participants was transcribed. Ordinary English orthography was used to transcribe the utterances of the adults and, where possible, the utterances of the children; where this was not possible, a conventional transcription of the children's utterances was made.

The children's utterances were then coded, using the coding system described below. Coding was carried out by using the transcribed conversation and the videorecording in conjunction.

All utterances spoken by the child during a session were coded or were scored as "not possible to categorize".

The coding system evolved with continued observation: some distinctions were refined and some discarded, but a set of working definitions that bear a reasonable resemblance to the system described evolved rapidly from my first attempt at a system of categorization. The system is designed to operate at a number of levels. At a first-order level it describes the general functions for which the children used language. The main functions (defined below) were: Regulation, Statement, Exchange, Personal and Conversation. These functions are regarded as descriptive conveniences. They each subsume a number of more specific categories. These categories are the second-order level of the system and they represent the specific functions for which the children used language. At this level of description the system is designed to capture the intended meaning of the utterance as judged by the relation of the utterance to the verbal and non-verbal context, the intonation of the utterance, and any consequences of the utterance and its uptake that further clarify the initial intention. The level of description is approximately that of a speech-act. At a third-order level the system can be further subdivided into the specific lexical and structural means used to realize particular speech-acts.

The system is not limited to the presence of words. Utterances that do not contain recognizable words can be used for effective, if limited, communication by the child as Halliday (1975) and some earlier writers (e.g. Lewis, 1936) have shown. Thus, the system to be proposed is, at the second-order level, a specification of the intentionally recognizable vocal communications of children. The basis on which an utterance is categorized is its communicative intent (and similarly the basis on which an utterance is adjudged "not possible to categorize" is inability to discern any particular communicative intent in that utterance). The system covers the range of communicative behaviours engaged in by the children during the period studied. Two points are of some importance in relation to these communicative behaviours. The first is that different communicative behaviours require different degrees of linguistic skill for their successful accomplishment and therefore some speech-acts, rarely, if ever, occurred during the early part of the period studied. The second point is that a particular speech-act may be expressed by different linguistic means at different points in time. The way in which the linguistic realization of a particular communicative intention changed over time is the focus of the third-order level of analysis, which will be reported in the results of the study. The categorization system at the first- and second-order levels is described below with illustrative examples where necessary. The categories are not, in general, mutually exclusive. An utterance was categorized in two categories if it fulfilled the criteria of both. It was not specified in advance which combinations were permissible, although some combinations were excluded by definition, as where two categories differentiate between two alternative interpretations of an utterance. The reason for the lack of specificity of permissible overlap was the desire to determine empirically what overlaps occurred in communicative behaviour.

4.2 The Regulation categories

This set of categories includes utterances that attempt to regulate the behaviour of another person in some way.[1]

Attention: an utterance that attempts to direct the attention of another person to some object, action, or event. Utterances in this category are frequently accompanied by pointing. If the child points to an object and looks from the object to another person while vocalizing in an attempt to direct that person's attention, the utterance is categorized as Attention. Calling the other person's name, saying *look*, or naming the object while pointing would all be categorized as Attention (the last could also be categorized as Naming – see below).

Request: an utterance that requests or demands that another person do something or get something for the child or that requests permission from another person to do something. These utterances typically have a characteristic rising intonation. If the child reaches

[1] Occasionally, family pets and toys such as dolls and teddy bears were addressed by the children. To avoid cumbersome definitions it is intended that everything that applies to persons can equally apply to pets or playthings in appropriate circumstances. Although the way in which children address pets or playthings is of interest in its own right, any such utterances in this study were coded in terms of their communicative function as if they had been addressed to persons.

for an object or attempts to enlist aid in some activity and insistently vocalizes while doing so, the utterance is categorized as Request. Thus a child might request more juice in any of the following ways: by saying *more*; by appealing to the requestee: *mummy*; by specifying what is requested: *juice*.

Vocative: an utterance that calls to another person either to locate the person or to request the person's presence. Vocative utterances are distinguished from Request utterances by the fact that it is the person's presence, not his or her aid, that is requested.

4.3 The Statement categories

This set of categories includes utterances that make some statement about the child's environment.

Naming: an utterance that makes reference to an object or person by name only. The paradigm case is where a child uses a name to label an object. However, there are also a number of more problematic uses of names that are here distinguished from labelling.

(a) Onomatopoeia: utterances such as *woof* or *moo* when it is not clear from the context if the child intends the utterance to be a label for the animal or object.

(b) Interaction: names observed to be used while interacting with a person or animate object. This is characteristic of the early stages of one-word use. The motivation for separating these utterances from labelling derives from the observations of Halliday (1975) who drew attention to the interactive function that names sometimes serve.

(c) Association: names uttered in the absence of the referent but in the presence of some object, person, location, etc. associated with the referent. Thus, *daddy*, uttered in association with a possession of daddy's, is regarded as Association. Cases of apparent over-extension of a referent are not regarded as instances of Association.

Description: an utterance that makes some statement, other than naming or in addition to naming, about an object, action, or event. The topic on which comment is passed may be explicit in the utterance, as it is in *ball gone*, but it need not be – *gone* in the appropriate context would also be categorized as Description. There is a large variety of possible descriptions including comments on actions, attributes, recurrence, non-existence and location of objects. Thus, the following utterances would all be categorized as Description: *allgone*, said on the disappearance of an object; *more car*, on seeing another car; *hit up sky*, on observing somebody throw an object high into the air; *like bus*, on comparing some object to a bus; *there*,[2] specifying the location of an object; *daddy coat*, specifying the owner of a coat; *chair*, specifying the location of some other object on the chair. There are two restrictions on the Description category: the utterance must describe some aspect of the immediate situation (this distinguishes Description from Information) and the description must not relate to an action that the child has carried out or intends to carry out. Utterances of the latter types will be discussed under the Personal categories as Doing and Determination respectively.

Information: an utterance that makes a statement about some event beyond the here-and-now, either an event that has happened or that will or could happen (but excluding utterances that specify the child's intention to act in the immediate future – see Determination). In the following exchange the child's utterances would be categorized as Information:

> Mother: *What did you have to eat on the train yesterday?*
> Child: *Apples.*
> M: *And what else?*
> C: *Sandwiches.*

4.4 The Exchange categories

This set of categories includes utterances used in an exchange of objects between the child and another person.

---

[2] A note on *there*: *there* has an ambiguous locative/existential role in language use. Lyons (1967) has commented on the fact that existential and locative constructions are closely related in general and have a common locative basis in many languages. Any locative/existential use of *there* was categorized as Description. The possible uses of *there* are not exhausted by this: it can be used in giving an object to another person (*there* = "there you are" – see Giving below), and it can be used to specify the completion of an activity (*there* = "there, I've done it" – see Doing below).

Giving: an utterance spoken while giving or attempting to give an object to another person. The successful accomplishment of giving is not a necessary condition – the child's attempt may be ignored by the other and the act may fail. If an object is exchanged and the utterance specifies (either intonationally or lexically) that the recipient is intended to do something with the object then the utterance is categorized as Request, not Giving. *Here, there, ball* (without rising intonation, while exchanging a ball) would be categorized as Giving. In the same context *play, ball* (with rising intonation) or *more* (assuming previous activity) would be categorized as Request.

Receiving: an utterance spoken while receiving an object from another person (e.g. *thanks*).

4.5 The Personal categories

This set of categories includes utterances that describe or express the child's own actions, states, feelings, or intentions.

Doing: an utterance that describes an action that the child is carrying out or has just carried out (but not actions that he or she intends to carry out – see Determination). This category is comparable to the subset of descriptions that describe the actions of others. Examples: the child says *up* while climbing onto a chair, *down* having got down from a chair, *there* having completed some action, *kick ball* having kicked a ball.

Determination: an utterance that expresses the child's intention to carry out some action immediately. Examples: the child says *again* before repeating some action, *up* before starting to climb up, *drink* before proceeding to get a drink. This category is comparable to the Request category; it relates to the child's regulation of his or her own behaviour while Request relates to the regulation of the behaviour of others.

Refusal: an utterance spoken to refuse to do something, accept something, or otherwise accede to the wishes of another.

Protest: a high-pitched utterance expressing the child's displeasure with some event or some action by another person.

4.6 The Conversation categories

This set of categories is fundamentally different from the others, as it is concerned with the relations between utterances produced by different speakers. In conversation an utterance can be of two sorts: it can either be a response to a preceding utterance or it can be the first utterance of a conversational sequence. The two types of utterance are called respectively 'conversational responses' and 'conversational initiations'.

Conversational responses generally have a close contiguous relation to the preceding utterance. However, any attempt to make some temporal interval t the operational limit within which conversational responses must begin runs into the twin objections that it excludes legitimate responses and includes illegitimate ones. An utterance that is a response to a preceding utterance may be legitimately delayed in time for a variety of reasons; a response may require some thought or time may elapse because of the nature of the initiating utterance: *tell me when it reaches 60* $(t_1 > t)$, *now*; *have you finished yet* $(t_2 > t)$, *yes*. Alternatively, the contiguous relation can sometimes be one of obvious chance, as when one participant does not attend to or fails to hear a preceding utterance but contiguously follows that utterance. These remarks are qualifications on what is generally true of conversational responses: that they bear a contiguous relation to the preceding utterance of the other party. They do so however because, in general, contiguity satisfies a requirement of participation. But that the essential criterion is participation rather than contiguity is demonstrated by the legitimate exceptions noted above.

In the present study an utterance was regarded as a conversational response if it was contiguous to the preceding utterance of the other party with the exception of a small number of utterances that clearly satisfied the conditions of either of the restrictions on contiguity noted above. Contiguity was not operationally defined. An intuitive criterion of what exceeded an acceptable pause limit was used. Interobserver reliability scores (see below) showed the intuitive judgements of different observers to be in good agreement. Two successive utterances would both be categorized as responses if the second utterance either repeated the first (possibly in the belief that the speaker had not heard or had not acknowledged the first response) or clarified it. Also important for purposes of analysis is the definition of an adult utterance. An adult utterance was defined as any period of connected speech followed by a pause of sufficient length to allow the child the possibility of taking a turn.

In coversation one participant must initiate the dialogue. The children's utterances frequently had the effect of initiating a conversation but it was, more often than not, impossible to determine whether they had intended to initiate conversation. The only clear case of the intentional initiation of conversation was when a child asked a question, and consequently Question is the only category of conversational initiation. Thus, although there will be some clear cases, apart from questions, of utterances intended to initiate conversation, these are not categorized in the present system.

Imitation: an utterance that imitates all or part of a preceding adult utterance and spoken in immediate response to that utterance. An utterance with a longer than usual pause by the child before imitating the preceding utterance would not be categorized as Imitation. Utterances in conversational exchanges, such as peek-aboo, that involve repeated use of a single utterance would not be categorized as Imitation but as Follow-on (see below).

Answer: an utterance spoken in response to a question, unless the utterance imitates the question or some word in the question. An adult question is regarded as an utterance with either Subject–Verb inversion, or containing a tag, and/or having question intonation.

Follow-on: an utterance that satisfies the criteria of a conversational response but is neither Imitation nor Answer.

Question: an utterance that requests information from another person.

4.7 The Miscellaneous category

This category consists of utterances where the child's intention is intelligible but the utterance cannot be categorized in any of the above categories. Examples of utterances that would be categorized as Miscellaneous are salutes (*hallo*, *bye-bye*) when the child initiates an interaction with a salute, and utterances that describe the child's mental states (*I believe...*, *I think...*, etc.). In principle, the system proposed above can be extended to include new categories, should sufficient numbers of miscellaneous examples warrant it.

4.8 Comparison with other categorization systems

A number of recent studies have proposed categorization systems for analysis of the utterances of children speaking one word at a time. This section compares the systems of Halliday (1975), Greenfield and Smith (1976), and Dore (1973, 1975) with the system proposed here.

4.8.1 *Halliday's system*

Halliday (1975) proposes that the child's first utterances each serve a single communicative function and that these functions are later combined so that each utterance becomes "effectively plurifunctional" (see 2.1.4 for a consideration of this theory). This section is concerned with the initial functions proposed by Halliday: the Instrumental, Regulatory, Interactional, Personal, Heuristic and Imaginative.

The Instrumental and Regulatory functions of Halliday's system are both request functions and are comparable to the Request category proposed here. Halliday distinguishes between utterances that request specific objects (Instrumental) and utterances that request specific behaviours (Regulatory). Although this distinction is not drawn here, it is one of potential use in studying the different varieties of requests that children make.

Halliday's Interactional function consists of "language used by the child to interact with those around him" (1975: 19). It subsumes a variety of utterances that would be distinguished as separate speech-acts by the present system: utterances used to call attention to objects (Attention); names used with a purely interactional function (the Interaction utterances of Naming); greetings (Miscellaneous); responses to calls (either Answer or Follow-on).

At first sight Halliday's Personal function appears to be somewhat similar to the Personal categories proposed here as he defines this function as

language used to express the child's own uniqueness; to express his awareness of himself, in contradistinction to his environment...This includes, therefore, expressions of personal feelings, of participation and withdrawal, of interest, pleasure, disgust and so forth.   (1975: 20)

However, an examination of the data on Halliday's son, Nigel, when he was approximately 16 months old (1975: 154–5) reveals that Halliday regards naming as falling within the Personal function, presumably on the basis that the names used are an expression of Nigel's interest although it is difficult to see in what way naming dogs, buses, and cars "expresses awareness of himself, in contradistinction to his environment".

The Heuristic function Halliday defines as "the demand for a name, which is the child's way of categorizing the objects of the physical world" (1975: 20). Any such utterances would be categorized as Question in the present system.

Halliday's Imaginative function (language used in pretend play and make-believe) is not included in the system proposed here because such use of language was rarely observed, due, in all probability, to the type of interactions observed. A number of categories used in the system proposed here are not comparable to any of the functions proposed by Halliday. This is due, in part, to the fact that Halliday's functions only cover the initial period of language development and in part to the different theoretical orientations of the systems.

4.8.2 *Greenfield and Smith's system*

It is difficult to compare directly the system of Greenfield and Smith with the system proposed here. In Greenfield and Smith's system utterances are categorized on the basis of semantic content whereas in the present system utterances are categorized on the basis of communicative intent. The ways of semantically expressing any particular communicative intention in a one-word utterance are various. For example, utterances categorized as Request in the present system would be distributed across several categories in

Greenfield and Smith's system. The semantic distinctions between utterances that Greenfield and Smith draw, are not, however, irrelevant to the present system. The different ways in which utterances *within* a category of the present system can be semantically expressed will be discussed in the analysis of the results of the present study. Thus, some of Greenfield and Smith's distinctions will be applicable at the third-order level of the present system. However, any similarities that exist indicate only that the systems are in some agreement on how semantic distinctions should be drawn. The present system has no commitment to the "underlying structure" of semantic content proposed by Greenfield and Smith.

The principal categories proposed by Greenfield and Smith are: Performative, Volition, Indicative Object, Volitional Object, Agent, Action or State of an Agent, Action or State of an Object, Object, Dative, Object Associated with Another Object or Location, Animate Being Associated with Object or Location, Location, and Modification of an Event. These categories will be discussed in turn.

Performatives are defined by Greenfield and Smith as "utterances that occur as part of a child's action" (1976: 50); *hi* and *bye-bye* are examples. These utterances would be categorized in either the Miscellaneous category or in one of the Conversation categories in the present system, depending on whether the utterance initiated an exchange of salutes or was a response to a salute by another person. Greenfield and Smith regard such utterances as performatives because they fulfil Austin's (1962) criterion of being subject to felicity conditions rather than truth conditions, and they regard these utterances as "the ontogenetic basis of later Performatives" (1976: 51). Austin's performative verbs include such verbs as 'promise', 'bet' and 'approve'. Greenfield and Smith do not make it clear if *hi* and *bye-bye* are supposed to be the ontogenetic basis of verbs such as these. The possibility seems quite remote.

Utterances categorized as Volition by Greenfield and Smith are those utterances whose "basic function is to obtain some desired response from the person addressed. The most common examples of this category are *mama*, used to request something, and *no*, used to reject something" (1976: 51). These utterances would be categorized as Request and Refusal respectively in the present system. Greenfield and Smith also regard utterances such as *yes* as examples of Volition in contexts such as the following:

Matthew whines *fishy*, pointing in their direction; his mother responds *Do you want to see the fish?* and he answers *yeah*, thus expressing positive Volition or desire.   (1976: 100)

This utterance would be categorized as Answer in the present system. The example illustrates a decided peculiarity in Greenfield and Smith's method of categorization. The response *yes* would be a typical and appropriate response to such a question from any speaker of the English language and the utterance can be simply described as an affirmative answer to a question. The fact that *fishy* would be categorized by Greenfield and Smith as Volitional Object does not mean that *yes*, which confirms the interpretation of *fishy* as a Volitional utterance, also expresses Volition.

Utterances categorized as Indicative Object in Greenfield and Smith's system would be categorized as Naming in the present system, and utterances categorized as Volitional Object would be categorized as Request in the present system.

According to Greenfield and Smith (1976: 54) "an Agent is "the typically animate perceived instigator" of an action (Fillmore 1968, p. 24)". They offer the following example: "if a child hears someone coming and says *dada*, *dada* is an Agent" (1976: 54). In the present system *dada* would be categorized as an associative instance of Naming – the footsteps are associated with the child's father.

The categories Action or State of an Agent and Action or State of an Object are self-explanatory. In the present system the utterances so categorized by Greenfield and Smith would, in most cases, be categorized as Description; however, if the child was the agent in question the utterance would be categorized as Doing. Even so, the overlap between the two systems is not complete. In discussing Action or State of an Object, Greenfield and Smith offer the following example:

At Nicky IV – 20(23), Nicky expresses negative Action or State for the first time by responding *no* to a statement or question from his mother.

In one example, Nicky's mother asks him *Does that one go in there?* (referring to an inlaid puzzle piece) and he replies *no*. (1976: 135)

It is a somewhat incredible claim that *no* in such circumstances contains any actual or potential semantic specification of an action or state. In the present system Nicky's utterance would be categorized as Answer.

Greenfield and Smith categorized a word as Object if the object referred to "was decisively involved in an action that changed its state or otherwise directly affected it" (1976: 56). In the present system a word that described some aspect of an action (in this case the object-acted-upon) would be categorized as Description. Other instances of Object in Greenfield and Smith's system, such as *fan* uttered to request that a fan be turned on would be categorized as Request in the present system.

The Dative in Greenfield and Smith's system includes the following: recipient of an object – for example (p. 140), Matthew "offers a bottle to his father and says *dada*" – Giving in the present system; beneficiary of an action – for example (p. 141), "Matthew says *yaya* (Lauren) when he pours yoghurt in the kitchen and repeats it as he walks into the dining room to his sister Lauren" – Determination in the present system; experiencer of a perception – for example (p. 57), the utterance *I see* – no specific category in the present system, therefore Miscellaneous; and "animate correlates to the objective case" (p. 56) – for example (p. 140), "Nicky says *han(d)* when he wants his wet hands dried" – Request in the present system. As Greenfield and Smith remark "there is room for serious doubt about whether or not the case has cognitive unity" (p. 56).

Utterances that Greenfield and Smith categorized as Object Associated with Another Object or Location, and Animate Being Associated with Object or Location would both be categorized as associative instances of Naming in the present system. Utterances categorized as Location in their system would be categorized as Description in the present system. (Utterances that describe the spatial position or orientation of an object form a subcategory of Description in the present system and the two systems are thus in basic agreement on the categorization of utterances describing location.)

Modification of an Event is defined by Greenfield and Smith as "a word that modifies an entire event rather than a single element" (1976: 59). As examples: "Matthew says *again* to mean that he wants his mechanical train wound again" (p. 59) – this utterance would be categorized as Request in the present system; an utterance such as *back myself*, uttered when Matthew was about to put a duck-piece back in a puzzle (p. 156) would be categorized as Determination in the present system; an utterance such as *too big* uttered after Nicky had tried unsuccessfully to balance a postcard on top of a toy (p. 155) would be categorized as Description in the present system. The differences in theoretical orientation between the two systems thus lead to a considerable lack of overlap in the categories of one system with that of the other.

4.8.3 *Dore's system*

The remaining system of categorization to be considered is that advanced by Dore (1973, 1975). He proposes that the speech-act be adopted as the basic unit of analysis of one-word utterances. The comparison between the present system and Dore's system is therefore relatively straightforward. Dore identified the following speech-acts:

Labelling: the child utters a word and attends to the object or event – Naming in the present system.

Repeating: the child utters a word or prosodic pattern in imitation of an adult utterance but does not address the adult or await a response from the adult – Miscellaneous in the present system.

Answering: the child utters a word in response to an adult utterance – either Imitation, Answer, or Follow-on in the present system.

Requesting Action: the child utters a word or marked prosodic pattern addressed to an adult and awaits a response – Request in the present system.

Requesting Answer: the child utters a word addressed to an adult and awaits a response. Dore (1975: 32) offers the example of a child picking up a book, looking at her mother and saying *book* with a rising intonation. This utterance would be categorized as Question in the present system, but there is no category for any other type of addressed remark in the present system.

Calling: the child calls an adult – Vocative in the present system.

Greeting: the child utters a greeting – Miscellaneous in the present system, unless uttered in response to an adult utterance, in which case either Imitation, Answer, or Follow-on.

Protesting: the child utters a word or marked prosodic pattern while resisting or denying an adult's action – either Refusal or Protest in the present system.

Practising: the child utters a word or prosodic pattern that is not addressed to an adult and no apparent aspect of the context is relevant to the utterance – such utterances would not be categorized in the present system.

The system of categorization proposed here is more detailed than Dore's system in that it includes the categories of Attention, Description, Information, Giving, Receiving, Doing and Determination, which have no counterpart in Dore's system. Part of the reason is that the present system is designed to include early multi-word utterances, as well as one-word utterances, to which Dore's system was restricted; in addition, the present system is a more detailed description of the speech-acts carried out with one-word utterances.

5

A longitudinal study of language development between 1 and 2 years old

5.0 Reliability of the categorization system

All of the children's utterances with a recognizable intentional meaning were categorized using the system described in Chapter 4. Utterances that could not be categorized were scored as such. No utterances were omitted from the analysis that follows. The children's utterances did not always consist of words, particularly in the earlier months of the study. A distinction was therefore made between utterances that contained identifiable words and utterances that contained no identifiable words. The former are called 'lexicalized utterances' and the latter are called 'non-lexicalized utterances'.

In order to establish the reliability of the categorization system two independent judges each categorized sequences of 100 consecutive utterances. Judge A categorized a sequence for each child when the children's speech consisted predominantly of words and most of the categories might reasonably be expected to be brought into use. Judge B categorized a sequence for four of the children when their utterances consisted predominantly of non-words and many of the utterances might thus be expected to contain no recognizable intent. Thus, the scores from the two judges represent somewhat different aspects of reliability. The scores from Judge A represent agreement on the categorization of utterances that were mostly lexicalized. The scores from Judge B represent agreement on the categorization of utterances that were mostly non-lexicalized. The judges who performed the reliability studies were both practised and competent observers of children and both had an interest in the topic of language development. They were separately trained in the application of the categorization system by viewing a selection of tapes and discussing the categorization of these tapes with the author.

86

Each judge's categorization of a sequence of 100 utterances was compared with that of the author. Due to the complexity of the system of categorization the judges sometimes made mistakes by forgetting to apply a particular category. Consequently author and judge discussed whether a mistake had been made or whether a disagreement existed. Mistakes were recategorized by the judge and the revised categorization was used to determine the reliability score.[1] As can be seen from Table 2 there was good agreement between the author and the judges in the application of the categorization system.

TABLE 2. *Percentage agreement of independent judges with the author's categorization*

	Child					
Judge	Alice	Brian	Carol	David	Emily	Fiona
A	97	98	93	93	90	90
B	—	92	87	91	90	—

5.1 General quantitative results

The proportion of utterances that were lexicalized and the utterance rate per 30 minutes (the modal length of a recording session) are shown in Figure 2 for each child for each observation.[2] The proportion of lexicalized utterances increased over time, a not unexpected result. In general the number of utterances tended to increase also – the children talked more, and more of their talk was intelligible as they grew older. There are exceptions to this general pattern. In Brian's case utterance rate was declining towards the end of the second year, but this is due entirely to the fact that in

---

[1] It occasionally (but rarely) transpired that a disagreement was due to a mistaken categorization on the author's part. Any such mistakes were not allowed for in calculating reliabilities, unlike the judges' mistakes, although the categorization was corrected before further analysis.

[2] In Figure 2, and all subsequent figures and tables where data are reported on a monthly basis, ages are recorded to the last full month. Thus, all entries in the columns headed '12' are derived from observations carried out between the ages of 12 and 13 months.

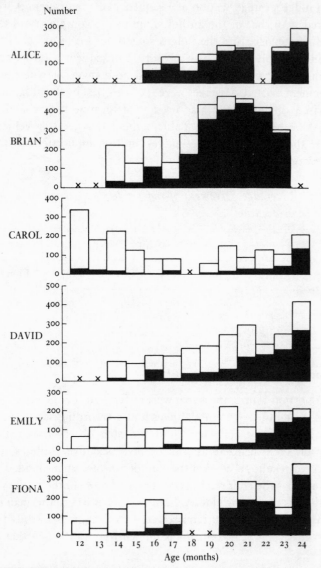

Figure 2. Utterance rate per 30 minutes for lexicalized and non-lexicalized utterances. ■ Lexicalized utterances; □ non-lexicalized utterances; × no observation at this age

his case the mean length of utterance had increased considerably by the age of 2; it is certainly not the case that he had ceased to be the most loquacious of the children. The other notable exception is Carol, who had a high utterance rate initially, which then declined steadily before making something of a recovery towards the end of the second year. There is no ready explanation for this; it can merely be recorded that it occurred.

Lexicalized and non-lexicalized utterances differed in the extent to which they were communicative. The average proportion of communicative lexicalized utterances was 0.92 while the average proportion of communicative non-lexicalized utterances was only 0.32. However, these proportions must be considered in the light of the data in Figure 2. In the earlier months of the study the vast majority of the children's utterances were non-lexicalized and thus, even though a higher percentage of lexicalized utterances were communicative, the majority of communication was initially carried out by the use of non-lexicalized utterances.

In order to determine whether there was a significant trend in the transition from non-lexicalized to lexicalized utterances in conveying communicative intent, the proportion of communicative utterances that were lexicalized was computed for each child for each month and these proportions were correlated with age. The resulting values of r were: 0.65 ($p < 0.05$), 0.92 ($p < 0.001$), 0.70 ($p < 0.02$), 0.87 ($p < 0.001$), 0.87 ($p < 0.001$), 0.90 ($p < 0.001$) for Alice, Brian, Carol, David, Emily, and Fiona respectively. The lowest correlation, that for Alice, is due to a "ceiling effect". No data were available prior to the age of 16 months, and by 16 months the proportion of communicative utterances that were lexicalized was 0.84 in her case.

The high correlations justify the fitting of linear regression lines to determine the rate of change of the proportion of communicative utterances that were lexicalized. The linear regressions are plotted in Figure 3 for five of the children. The data from Alice were not included in this plot because of the ceiling effect discussed above. The regression lines for Brian, David, Emily, and Fiona are remarkably similar suggesting a similar rate of change from non-lexicalized to lexicalized communicative utterances but a difference in onset time. The regression line for Carol suggests an

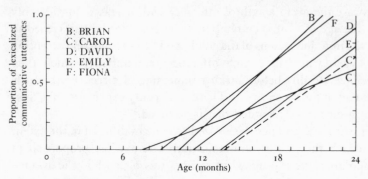

Figure 3. Regression lines for proportion of lexicalized communicative utterances on age

early onset of lexicalized communicative utterances but a slower rate of change. The early onset in this case is due to the high proportion of imitations in Carol's speech in the early months of the second year. If her regression line is based on the data from 19 months onwards, when the proportion of communicative utterances that consisted of imitations had fallen dramatically, then it is similar to the other four lines of regression as shown by the dotted line in Figure 3.

These results show that communicative intent does not depend on the learning of words for its initial expression, and the findings support the arguments of earlier chapters that the development of the intention to communicate is the basis of language development. Just which communicative intentions were present in the earlier months of the second year and which developed later will emerge from a more detailed consideration of the different communicative categories.

5.2 The Regulation categories

These categories contain those utterances that the children used to attempt to regulate the behaviour of another person in some way: by drawing or directing attention to some object, action, or event; by making some request for an object, action, or event; or by requesting the presence of another person by calling that person.

5.2.1 *Attention*

Utterances in this category served to draw or direct the attention of another person to some object, action, or event. The majority of these utterances were lexicalized utterances as can be seen from Figure 4. When the children used lexicalized utterances to direct the attention of another person they invariably used utterances of one of four types: they either said *look*, or *that*, or they used the name of the object to which they were directing attention, or they used the name of the person whose attention they were attempting to direct. The only other lexicalized utterances used by a child to direct attention were all of the form *see X*, where *X* specified what was to be seen. Table 3 shows how often each child used each utterance-type. Utterances that contained more than one word were categorized according to the word in the child's utterance that served to direct attention. Thus, *look ball* or *look mummy* would both be categorized under *look* rather than under Name of Object or Name of Person.

It can be seen from Table 3 that not all utterance-types occurred with equal frequency. *Look* occurred with greatest frequency and was used by all of the children on at least some occasions. In order to determine whether the ordering of the children's utterance-types for directing attention was statistically significant a Friedman analysis of variance by ranks was performed. The relative ordering of utterance-types by ranks, for the group as a whole, was *Look*, Name of Person, *That*, Name of Object, and Other. The analysis of variance indicated a significant ordering of preference, $\chi_r^2(4) = 13.7$, $p < 0.01$.

It is noticeable that object names were rarely used to direct attention. Bates *et al.* (1975) have claimed that naming and directing attention are related behaviours. The children in this study used names only on rare occasions for the purpose of directing attention. This finding suggests that there is little relation between naming and directing attention. It does not, of course, suggest that the capacity for joint attention is not a psychological prerequisite for the development of naming. It is compatible with this result that the development of naming occurs most readily in a context where mother and child are jointly attending to objects.

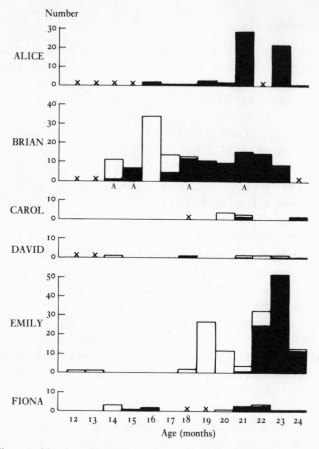

Figure 4. Number of lexicalized and non-lexicalized Attention utterances (A = average score from two observations). For key see Figure 2

However, when joint attention did not exist but was required by these children, they rarely used the names of objects to achieve such joint attention. The differences in the speech strategies used to name objects and to draw attention to them was particularly evident in the case of Emily. Prior to the observation session at 22 months Emily had only been observed to use one lexicalized utterance to direct attention. However, during the observations at 22 months and 23 months Emily used *look* frequently while looking at a picture-book with her mother. Emily mainly did one of two

TABLE 3. *Distribution of lexicalized Attention utterances*

Child	*Look*	*That*	Name of Object	Name of Person	Other
			Subcategory		
Alice	21 (6)	11 (0)	3 (2)	6 (1)	0 (0)
Brian	81 (32)	1 (1)	0 (0)	27 (4)	5 (5)
Carol	3 (0)	0 (0)	0 (0)	1 (0)	0 (0)
David	3 (1)	0 (0)	1 (0)	0 (0)	0 (0)
Emily	79 (2)	8 (1)	0 (0)	3 (0)	0 (0)
Fiona	4 (2)	0 (0)	1 (0)	6 (0)	0 (0)
Total	191 (43)	20 (2)	5 (2)	43 (5)	5 (5)

Note. Numbers in parentheses indicate the number of utterances that contained two or more words.

things while looking at the picture-book: she named the object if she knew its name or she said *look* to draw attention to what she was interested in on a particular page. Emily's use of these two utterance-types differed in the following way. Naming was an end in itself, no further utterance was required from her mother to complete that particular exchange. *Look*, on the other hand, was both a demand that her mother attend and a call for conversational participation from her mother. If her mother did not respond to Emily's *look*, the utterance was frequently repeated and the exchange completed by the mother naming the object. In this case, the sharing of attention and the behaviour of naming, within the dyad, were closely related but distinct activities; *look* was used to call attention and names were used to name objects.

A point of some interest is the word combinations the children used to direct attention. Most studies of two-word combinations have concentrated exclusively on the syntactic or semantic structure of descriptive utterances. The combinations that occurred in utterances used to direct attention reflect pragmatic rather than syntactic or semantic relations. The most common combination was *look* uttered in conjunction with the name of the person called to attend (60 per cent of all combinations in this category). The use of an address term is a powerful turn-allocation technique in conversation (Sacks *et al.*, 1974) and the prevalence of Attention utterances with an address term reflects the development of conversational and communicative skills. The words do not directly qualify each other as words would in descriptive utterances; rather, one word commands attention and the other addresses the command to a specific person.

5.2.2 *Request*

Utterances in this category were requests or demands that another person do something or get something for the child (or requests for permission from another person to do or get something). It is clear, from Figure 5, that the children could request with efficacy before they had learnt to utter words to request. For much of the second year lexicalized and non-lexicalized requests coexisted with the balance gradually shifting towards lexicalized requests. The proportion of lexicalized requests was positively correlated with age; $r = 0.64$ ($p < 0.05$), 0.94 ($p < 0.001$), 0.48 ($p < 0.05$), 0.94 ($p < 0.001$), 0.74 ($p < 0.003$), 0.94 ($p < 0.001$) for Alice, Brian, Carol, David, Emily, and Fiona respectively. Lexicalized requests were subcategorized as follows:

Person: the child used a person's name to request him or her to do something. If the child used a person's name to identify the addressee and additionally made a specific request of the addressee, then the utterance was categorized according to the request specified.

Recurrence: the child requested either that something be repeated or that he or she be given more of something.

Object: the child requested some object specified by name or requested that something be done to an object specified by name.

Action: the child requested that some specified action be performed. Requests that specified both the object and the action were categorized according to the word that occurred first.

Forbidding: the child forbade another person to carry out some action or ordered another person to cease some action.

Conventional Mood: the child used a conventional grammatical means of signalling that the utterance was a request, such as *I*

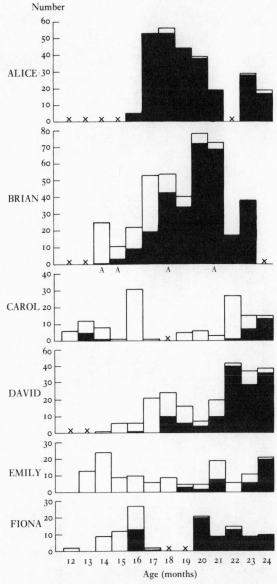

Figure 5. Number of lexicalized and non-lexicalized Request utterances
(A = average score from two observations). For key see Figure 2

TABLE 4. *Distribution of lexicalized Requests*

| | | | | Subcategory | | Conventional | |
Child	Person	Recurrence	Object	Action	Forbidding	Mood	Other
Alice	98 (0)	50 (19)	51 (12)	26 (10)	14 (0)	3 (3)	15 (6)
Brian	36 (1)	28 (12)	107 (10)	142 (90)	49 (22)	27 (27)	29 (9)
Carol	6 (0)	0 (0)	0 (0)	6 (1)	6 (2)	0 (0)	9 (1)
David	6 (1)	17 (0)	39 (0)	53 (12)	6 (1)	3 (3)	12 (2)
Emily	12 (0)	3 (0)	17 (0)	3 (2)	0 (0)	0 (0)	4 (0)
Fiona	6 (1)	12 (0)	0 (0)	13 (11)	10 (4)	32 (32)	3 (0)
Total	164 (3)	110 (31)	214 (22)	243 (126)	85 (29)	65 (65)	72 (18)

Note. Numbers in parentheses indicate the number of utterances that contained two or more words.

want... or *Can I*.... *Please*, used in isolation, was not categorized as Conventional Mood but as Other.

Other: any other lexicalized utterance used to request.

Table 4 reveals that all of the children sometimes used the name of the person they were interacting with in order to request that person to do something. As the observations were mostly of mother–child pairs, *mummy* was thus the most frequent utterance used. In many observations *mummy* was only observed to be used to perform the speech-act of requesting, and it is possible that *mummy* was initially learnt as a means of requesting from a particular person rather than as a name for that person. In most cases it was impossible to draw definite conclusions on this point, as restriction of a word to a particular speech-act during one half-hour of observation does not show that a child cannot use the word in other ways. However, conclusions could be drawn in the case of Alice. Alice used *mummy* between 16 and 20 months as a means of requesting from her mother and from the author during observation sessions (Alice frequently involved the author in her games). Alice was never observed to use *mummy* as a name for her mother during these sessions. Alice's use of *mummy* was not restricted to requests. She used it to call attention, to protest, and also while giving objects to her mother or to the author. The common feature of these situations was the involvement of other people in some joint action with Alice. From 20 months onwards Alice was never observed to use *mummy* in any of these ways again and it seemed that the word had now been "reclassified" as a name by Alice as she used it on several occasions at 20 months to name a mother in a picture-book.

Brian also displayed some initial consistency in the utterances used to request. Up to 17 months many of his requests were performed by uttering *eheheh* with a high pitch. At 17 months he replaced *eheheh* by *dah* which he used for almost all non-lexicalized requests on this occasion of observation. The other most common utterance used to request on this occasion was *dada* which Brian used to request from his father. It is possible that *dah* was an abbreviated form of *dada* but a number of factors weigh against this interpretation. Brian's use of *dah* was not restricted to his father, his use of *dada* was. Furthermore Brian's only request longer than one word at 17 months involved the combination of *dada* and *dah*. From 18 months onwards most of Brian's requests were lexicalized and consistent non-lexicalized forms were never observed again.

The utterances subcategorized as Recurrence are predominantly accounted for by *more* – the remaining small minority being accounted for by *again* and an occasional *another*. *More* had two uses in the children's speech: to request and to describe (for descriptive uses of *more* see 5.3.2). Up to 19 months *more* was used by Alice only to request, it was never used descriptively. From 20 months onwards she also used *more* descriptively and from that time onwards she used *more* in combination with other words in requests. *More* was first used by Brian at 20 months when he used it to both describe and request. Carol never used *more* at all during the observation sessions. David's first observed use of *more*, at 18 months, was to request; he was not observed to use it again until 21 months, at which time he used it to both describe and request. Emily only used *more* during one observation session (at 21 months) and she used it to both describe and request. Fiona, at 16 months, used *more* to both describe and request but did not use it to request in any of the other observations.

Five of the six children thus learnt an appropriate way to both request and describe recurrence. With Alice and David *more* was only observed initially in the context of requesting. With Brian, Emily, and Fiona an awareness of the semantic content of the word was evident in their first observed uses, as the word was not functionally restricted in the same way as it was for Alice and David. It follows from this that some children may initially learn some words to perform a particular speech-act and only later come to learn the independence of meaning and function (or, in Gricean terms, the difference between utterer's meaning and semantic meaning) while others may initially learn the same words as words with a particular meaning, which can be used in any context where the meaning is appropriate.[3]

Object words were used by four of the children to request and

---

[3] Needless to say, every word will be first used to perform some particular speech-act. The distinction drawn between the two sorts of learning is based on restriction to a particular functional use over an extended period of time.

action words were used by all six (although Carol and Emily were only observed to use action words to request during one observation session each). Object words were used in two main ways by the children: to request that they be given the object concerned, or to request that something be done to or with the object – for example, Brian held out a cup saying *cup* to demand that he be given a drink in the cup. Table 4 reveals that Alice, Brian, and David frequently used both object and action words to request. Their requests using these words were always appropriate; an object or action word was never observed to be used when the particular object or action specified was not in some way involved in the request. Thus, from the beginning, the children's lexicalized requests were characterized by their appropriateness. *Mummy* was used across a variety of situations involving a variety of objects and actions but, except in Alice's case, was always used to make a request from the mother; *more* was used to request a recurrence, and the recurrence could involve almost any object or action; specific object and action words were used only in situations where that object or action was requested and these words were never observed to be overextended during requesting. It is probable that at least some object and action words were initially restricted to use in requesting but this was difficult to determine because, as already stated, the observation of restricted use during one half-hour does not unequivocally show that a child cannot use the word in other speech-acts. More detailed records of a child's use of particular words would be necessary in order to resolve this issue. Anecdotal evidence from the mothers of the children in the study gives some support to the view that at least some object and action words were initially learnt as a means of performing the speech-act of requesting.

Forbidding was predominantly carried out by the use of *no*. All of Alice's forbidding consisted of *no* with the exception of four uses of *quiet* at 23 months to demand that the dog cease barking. Brian used both *no* and *not* to forbid; the only other utterance he used in this context was *stop it* which he used on three occasions at 21 months. All of Carol's forbidding consisted of *no*. David's first instance of forbidding, at 20 months, was *Fanah go away* spoken to the dog, all later instances were *no*. Fiona provided the most versatile range. At 21 months there were five instances of *don't*;

at 22 months one instance of *no* and one of *go away you*, at 23 months one instance of *don't hurt my fingers*, and at 24 months one instance of *don't touch it* and one of *leave it there*. With the exception of Fiona, the children's efforts to curtail the behaviour of other people were expressed predominantly by *no*.

Conventional Mood was expressed by the use of *want* followed by whatever it was that the children wanted. The only instance of Conventional Mood that did not involve *want* was Fiona's request at 24 months *can I have some more wood please?*

The only consistencies between the children in the use of utterances subcategorized as Other were that *please* was used by Alice, Carol, and Fiona and *mine* by Brian, Carol, and Fiona, the latter utterance being used to demand that some object be given to the child.

In summary, all of the children were capable of making successful requests without the use of lexicalized utterances, and some of them depended on this strategy for the majority of their second year. The communicative similarity of requesting in different situations was evidently recognized by the children who showed some consistency in the intonation and, at times, the phonology of their request utterances. There is obviously scope for more detailed and systematic exploration of the phonological and intonational consistency of non-lexicalized requests. The children gradually learnt to use the language they heard to make requests of both a general and a specific nature, and moreover their specific requests were invariably appropriate. By the time they were 2 years old some of the children displayed considerable semantic sophistication in the requests they were capable of making.

5.2.3 *Vocative*

Vocatives did not occur frequently (only 53 instances were recorded in the complete study) and when they did occur they always took the same form: the child called the mother's name in order to request her presence. There were no instances of non-lexicalized utterances categorized as Vocative.

5.3 The Statement categories

The speech-acts of these categories required conventional language for their successful performance. In order to name an object or to describe some property of an object or the action performed on or by an object it is necessary to produce an utterance that contains recognizable words. The fundamental difference between the speech-acts of the Regulation categories and those of the Statement categories is that the latter are not utilitarian in nature. Utterances in the Statement categories are the linguistic expression of the child's cognition of the world of objects and of other people. In order to express successfully the speaker's intention such utterances require conventional lexical content, whereas appropriate intonation is often sufficient to indicate a request regardless of the phonological or lexical content of the utterance. The differences go further. There are behavioural correlates of requesting and directing attention, such as reaching and pointing, which serve to further clarify the communicative intention of the speaker. The communicative intention of statements cannot be behaviourally disambiguated to the same extent.[4] A further difference between the two types of speech-acts is reflected in the fact that statements are subject to criteria of truth and falsity, whereas utterances that request and call attention are more appropriately considered as felicitous or infelicitous rather than as true or false.[5] Thus, with statements the burden of intelligibility is carried by the semantic content of the utterances. As far as children are concerned, the price of intelligibility of communicative intent when attempting to talk about the world is the adoption of the conventional means of doing so. The next three sections discuss how the children in this study learnt to do this.

[4] The term 'behavioural correlates' is meant to exclude systems of specialist use such as sign languages, which are linguistic substitutes rather than behavioural correlates. Of more interest is the use of gestures to accompany statements. Gestures rarely accompanied statements in this study, and when they did the semantics of statements had already developed to a considerable extent. Thus, gestures seem to follow rather than precede the semantic content of statements. For some speculation on this matter see McNeill (1975).

[5] The distinction between descriptive and non-descriptive utterances is not quite so simple, although it is sufficient for the present purpose. See Austin (1962), Katz (1977), Searle (1969), and Stampe (1975).

5.3.1 *Naming*

The category of Naming consists of words used to label an object, onomatopoeic sounds used to refer to an object, names used to interact with the person named, and names used to associate something with some absent referent. The frequency of occurrence of these different utterance-types is shown in Table 5.

TABLE 5. *Distribution of Naming utterances*

Child	Subcategory			
	Onomatopoeia	Interaction	Association	Labelling
Alice	18	18	11	330
Brian	6	7	4	395
Carol	1	0	0	38
David	45	5	10	170
Emily	11	0	45	118
Fiona	0	2	5	344
Total	81	32	75	1395

Onomatopoeia was most frequent in the cases of Alice, David, and Emily. With Alice and David these utterances occurred in the earlier months of the second year; with Emily in the later months. Most onomatopoeic utterances were animal sounds. Such utterances frequently contained a variable number of instances of the particular sound, a fact that, added to the inherent ambiguity of onomatopoeia, made it a methodological impossibility to decide whether such utterances were being used to label the object in question. Most of the objects that elicited onomatopoeia were conventionally named on later occasions.

Halliday (1975) has claimed that a child's initial use of a person's name often occurs in the context of interacting with that person. Where a child was observed to use a word in this way the utterance was subcategorized as Interaction. Alice, Brian, David and Fiona used words in this way on some occasions. Apart from Brian's *dada* (once at 14 months) and Fiona's *mama* (twice at 12 months) all other utterances in this category involved the children interacting with family pets.

Instances of Association were most common in the case of Emily. Associations involved the child saying the name of a particular referent while attending to some object, person, location, etc. associated with the referent. In Emily's case all instances of Association were accounted for by person names. The majority of her referential associations occurred during the last three observations, at 22, 23 and 24 months. Interestingly these occasions were also marked by her frequent use of *look*. Emily used *look* on these occasions to draw attention to a variety of objects. At this time she was clearly very interested in communicating about objects, but her principal means of communicating initially was either to draw attention to the object or to associate the object with a familiar person. Only during the last observation, at 24 months, did the instances of Labelling exceed the sum of the instances of Association and Attention.

The majority of utterances categorized as Naming were instances of Labelling. It was hypothesized in 2.2.6 that mastery of the concept of naming would be achieved by a relatively sudden realization (an insight) of the relationship between words already in use and the objects with which these words have been paired in certain ritual types of interaction between adult and child. Such mastery could be evidenced by a sudden increase in the size of the child's vocabulary of names. It was also hypothesized that, following insight into naming, words that describe actions and attributes would quickly follow, as would the development of structured utterances. The most appropriate test of these hypotheses would require complete details of vocabulary development. These details were not available to the author. On the basis of the data to hand (admittedly less than ideal), the number of different words used to label objects was computed and compared on a month-by-month basis with the number of different descriptions made and with the number of different structured utterances. Types rather than tokens were used in this analysis, as the hypotheses concern vocabulary growth and the development of grammatical structure. The results will be considered separately for each child.

Figure 6 shows the results for Alice. No data were obtained prior to 16 months. From 16 months onwards Alice was fond of looking at picture-books with her mother and this situation presented the

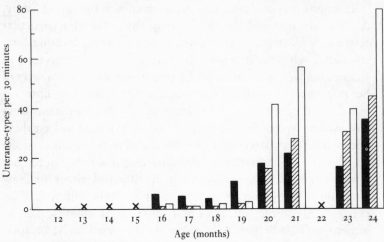

Figure 6. ALICE. ■ Labels; ▨ descriptions; □ structured utterances;
× no observation at this age

necessary interactive ritual for mastering the concept of naming.
A sudden increase in labelling was evident at 19 months, and in
descriptions and in structured utterances at 20 months. By 21
months labelling had ceased to constitute the majority of statements.
The data for Alice support the hypotheses advanced.

Figure 7 shows the results for Brian. No data were obtained prior
to 14 months. Like Alice, Brian frequently looked at picture-books
with his caretaker, so the necessary elements were present to test
the hypotheses advanced. A sudden increase in labelling, in
descriptions, and in structured utterances was evident at 19
months. (Descriptions increased in frequency at 18 months but
only to a relatively small total.) The relative frequency of labelling
fell sharply from 19 months onwards. The decrease in labelling
does not indicate that Brian ceased to learn names but that the
context in which names were observed had changed from one of
uttering the object's name to one of giving a more detailed
description of the object – that it was a *blue X, another Y*, and so
on. The data for Brian support the hypotheses advanced. The fact
that the three increases were evident during the same observation
was somewhat unexpected but may only reflect the relative rapidity
of Brian's language development.

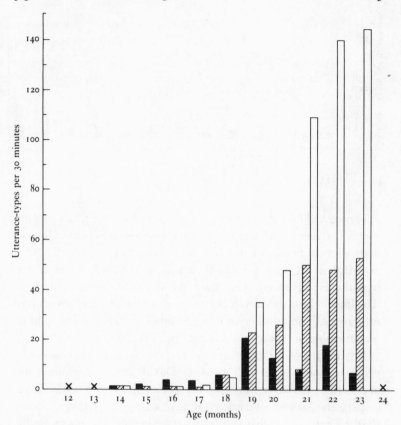

Figure 7. BRIAN. For key see Figure 6

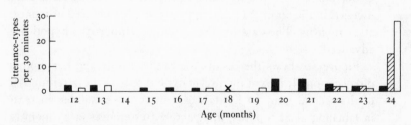

Figure 8. CAROL. For key see Figure 6

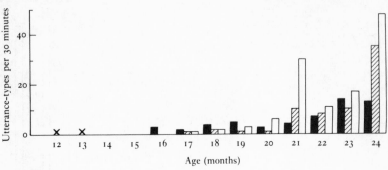

Figure 9. DAVID. For key see Figure 6

Figure 8 shows the results for Carol. In this case ritual naming games between Carol and her mother were never observed, either with picture-books or in any other situation. It is therefore doubtful if the data for Carol can be considered a test of the hypotheses advanced. Her data do show the development of labelling before the development of descriptions and structured utterances. The number of types is small in her case but it must be remembered that overall she had the lowest mean utterance rate.

Figure 9 shows the results for David. No data were obtained prior to the age of 14 months. David and his mother did occasionally look at picture-books together although David did not display the same enthusiasm for this activity as either Alice or Brian. There was a fairly sudden increase in labelling at 23 months. Unfortunately for the hypotheses advanced there was a sudden increase in the number of descriptions and of structured utterances at 21 months. The data for David do not support the hypotheses advanced.

Figure 10 shows the results for Emily. Emily and her mother did occasionally look at picture-books but only in the latter months of the second year. In Emily's case there was a sudden increase in labelling at 22 months, in structured utterances at 23 months, and in descriptions at 24 months. The data for Emily support the hypotheses advanced.

Figure 11 shows the results for Fiona. Fiona and her mother frequently looked at picture-books together. The necessary elements were therefore present to test the hypotheses advanced.

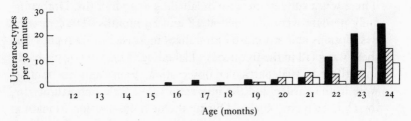

Figure 10. EMILY. For key see Figure 6

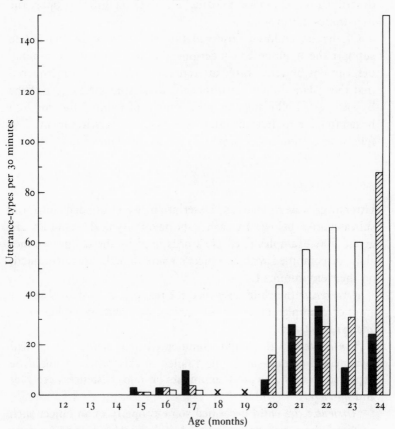

Figure 11. FIONA. For key see Figure 6

There was a sudden increase in labelling at 17 months. Unfortunately no data were obtained at 18 and 19 months. At 20 months descriptions and structured utterances increased in frequency but there was a fall in the frequency of labelling. This fall was probably an artifact of that particular observation. Fiona and her mother were in the garden and the interaction gave little opportunity for the child to name objects. During the next observation Fiona was back indoors and spent a considerable amount of time naming and describing objects in a catalogue. The data for Fiona support the hypotheses advanced.

Of the six children observed the data from only one fail to support the hypotheses concerning the development of naming, descriptions, and structured utterances (and it must be remembered that these data do not constitute the most appropriate test of the hypotheses). Following the development of naming the children began to learn to describe other aspects of their environment. The following section is concerned with this development.

5.3.2 *Description*

Utterances categorized as Description were divided into the subcategories below. In each subcategory typical examples are given. The examples cited are words used by the children either alone or combined with an object's name to make some comment on their environment.

Recurrence: the child described the reappearance of an object or another exemplar of an object, action, or event by saying *more*, *another*, or *again*.

Non-existence: the child commented that some object had disappeared or that some object failed to exist where it might be expected to exist. Typical comments on non-existence were *gone* and *no more*.

Attribute: the child described some property of an object such as state, colour, size, or quantity. Thus, *broke*, *blue*, *big* and *two* were subcategorized as Attribute.

Action: the child described the action that some person (except self) or object performed or was caused to perform, as for example, *hit*, *fall down*, *sit*.

Subject–Object: the child juxtaposed the names of two objects in order to describe some relationship (other than possession – see below) between the two. For example, the utterance *mummy shop* said to indicate that the mother in a story-book was going shopping, was subcategorized as Subject–Object.

Holophrase: the child used an object's name, on its own, to describe the object's role in some dynamic event. Thus, *daddy* to indicate that Daddy had acted, *ball* to indicate that the ball had rolled away, and *chair* to indicate that another object had been placed on the chair were subcategorized as Holophrase.

Comparison: the child compared one object to another by saying (*X is*) *like Y*.

Denial: the child denied that some proposition could be applied to a particular case (e.g. *not a ball*). Denial is distinguished from Non-existence in that Non-existence specifies the absence of something whereas Denial is a statement about the relationship between language and the world.

Possession: the child specified the possessor or owner of an object. If the utterance consisted of one word only (e.g. *daddy*), the utterance was subcategorized as Possession if it was clear from the context that possession or ownership was being specified. If this was not clear the utterance was subcategorized as Association in the Naming category.

Location: the child specified the location of an object by using a locative term such as *there, here, in, on, up, down*.

Other: any other utterances subsumed by the definition of Description but not falling into any of the subcategories above.

Where an utterance contained several words it was categorized according to what was judged to be the main theme of the description. There were few such utterances and, in context, judgement of the main theme was unproblematic. Table 6 reveals that the children learnt to make a wide range of comments on their environment, frequently in utterances that combined two or more words together. Word combinations invariably involved the name of the object together with some qualifying comment on the object. This fact, taken in conjunction with the findings on the initial prominence of naming, indicates that the children, having established a word–referent relationship between word and object, then

TABLE 6. *Distribution of Description utterances*

		Subcategory									
Child	Recurrence	Non-existence	Attribute	Action	Subject–Object	Holophrase	Comparison	Denial	Possession	Location	Other
Alice	11 (11)	16 (6)	60 (42)	32 (20)	12 (12)	8	7 (7)	4 (4)	2 (1)	42 (40)	9 (9)
Brian	63 (51)	92 (25)	149 (91)	123 (86)	5 (5)	44	0	2 (2)	24 (22)	164 (89)	14 (13)
Carol	0	2 (0)	13 (11)	5 (4)	0	0	0	0	8 (2)	3 (1)	0
David	6 (3)	33 (22)	19 (13)	40 (32)	0	4	0	0	5 (0)	23 (19)	2 (2)
Emily	1 (0)	7 (0)	14 (1)	8 (3)	0	3	0	0	8 (4)	9 (4)	0
Fiona	16 (15)	7 (4)	111 (104)	63 (56)	0	3	11 (11)	0	28 (27)	92 (84)	1 (1)
Total	97 (80)	157 (57)	366 (262)	271 (201)	17 (17)	62	18 (18)	6 (6)	75 (56)	333 (237)	26 (25)

Note. Number in parentheses indicate the number of utterances longer than one word.

began to realize that, if names name objects, other words specify the states, actions, etc. of objects and that these words can be combined with names to describe particular events and relationships. The features of events and relationships that were described by the children in this study have a general similarity to the conceptual relationships that characterize the achievements of sensorimotor intelligence in Piaget's theory and are thus consistent with the popular view that semantic relationships reflect conceptual relationships (Edwards (1973) is particularly relevant in this context).

Recurrence. Five of the children commented on recurrence (though only one instance was recorded in Emily's case). These utterances generally commented on another exemplar of a particular object-class (e.g. *more sheep*). These comments demonstrate the children's ability to categorize similar objects together, and the spontaneous occurrence of such comments demonstrates the children's motivation to seek similarities in the objects and events they encountered and to thus cognitively organize their environment. Comments on recurrence generally involved the use of *more* (occasionally *again* and *another*). The majority (82 per cent) of the children's comments on recurrence contained more than one word. Thus, the children generally specified the topic on which they were passing comment.

Non-existence. All of the children commented on the non-existence and disappearance of objects – typically by saying *gone* or *allgone* and occasionally by saying *no X* where X might be expected, as for example when Alice pointed to the eye-holes of her doll and said *no eyes*, or when Brian picked up a bald toy man and said *no hair*. Comments on non-existence indicate the children's sensitivity to the changes that occurred in their environment and thus indicate that this aspect of their environment was cognitively salient to the children. Comments on non-existence occurred more frequently as a single-word utterance than comments on recurrence did (64 per cent and 18 per cent respectively). The difference is instructive. An object that disappears disappears in its own right – it is simply gone. An object that exemplifies "moreness" does so only in relation to other similar objects, and thus a comment on recurrence contains at least an implicit reference to a class of objects. More often than not, as the results show, the children made the reference explicit.

Attribute. All of the children commented on the attributes of objects. Some attribute comments occurred as single-word utterances (particularly the earlier comments) but the majority (72 per cent) consisted of utterances involving word combinations. Comments on attributes included state descriptions (e.g. *happy, nice, sharp, broken*), quantity descriptions (e.g. *two, three* and, from Fiona only, *lots*), dimensional descriptions (e.g. *big, small, little* and, from Alice, *mummy* and *baby* as synonyms for 'big' and 'small' respectively), and colour descriptions.

The colour terms were the terms with which the children appeared to experience most difficulty in relating a particular word to a particular class. All of the children who used colour terms frequently made errors both by wrongly associating class and word and by overextending particular colour terms. Cruse (1977) in a study of the acquisition of colour terminology by one child has reported similar observations. The apparent difficulty in learning colour terms is one that calls for further experimental work in order to quantify the observation reported above. It seemed that both receptively and productively the children experienced difficulty with colour terms and their errors seemed to be random rather than systematic. An experimental investigation of children's understanding and use of colour terms would resolve whether or not the errors were random, and the understanding and use of other descriptive terms (e.g. state descriptions, dimensional descriptions) within a similar experimental paradigm would resolve whether or not colour terms are more difficult to learn than other terms. One reason for the apparent difficulty might be the following. Learning the class extension of a particular word may consist not merely in learning a list of features as Clark (1973) suggests but also in learning the relevant contrasts between closely related classes as Harrison (1972) suggests. Different animals would be examples of "closely related classes" and animal words were, in fact, sometimes over extended by the children in this study.[6] However a variety

---

[6] Some of the children made the following adjustment when told they were using an animal name incorrectly and supplied with the correct name: they incorporated the correct name into their vocabulary as an attribute-word (or possibly as a hyponym). Thus Brian, told that what he called *ducks* were turkeys, called the toys *turkey ducks*, and when told that

of potential cues exists for differentiating one animal class from another, such as relative size, outline shape, and sound and movement if the animals are live rather than toys. In the case of colour there is only one relevant contrast – colour itself, and it may be that restriction to a single dimension of contrast for a large variety of terms makes it a psychologically difficult task for children to learn colour terms.[7]

Action. Comments on the action of objects and of other people contained about the same proportion of utterances longer than one word as comments on attributes did (74 per cent and 72 per cent respectively). Thus, when the children commented on an action, they generally did so with an explicit reference to the person or object acting or acted upon. Findings reported by Goldin-Meadow, Seligman, and Gelman (1976) are relevant in this context. They tested vocabulary development of nouns and verbs during the second year by asking children *what's this?* and *what am I doing?* (or alternatively *what is the doll doing?*). They reported two stages of vocabulary development: a stage when the child responded with nouns but not verbs and a later stage when the child responded with both nouns and verbs. Thus, similarly to the present results, the production of verbs was found to occur later than the production of nouns.

Subject–Object. Subject–Object utterances were rare (1 per cent of all descriptions) and were only observed in the cases of Alice and Brian. It is not immediately apparent why such utterances should be so rare, but it may be that the juxtaposition of two nouns with some unspecified relationship serving as a link between them may demand a greater amount of information processing than the children are generally able or willing to do. Explanation of the cognitive organization that accounts for the production of such utterances is lacking at present. Bloom (1973) explained these

what he called *dog* was a cow, called the toy *cow dog*. Alice was also observed to make similar errors on a few occasions. The errors were never observed to persist from one session to the next so the children's interpretation appears to have only given rise to short-lived errors.

7 Colour terms are linguistically three-dimensional, viz. hue, saturation and luminosity. But this only adds to the child's problem of forming colour classes. My point above is that exemplars are often labelled *blue, green, red*, etc. for the child in the absence of any further possible contrasting information. Thus: *give me a blue bead; now a green one; now a red one;* and so on.

utterances by hypothesizing the "deletion" of the verb expressing the relationship between the subject and object. Such an explanation poses more problems than it answers (see 2.1.2), but a satisfactory alternative explanation has yet to be proposed.

Holophrase. Five of the children used holophrases on some occasions. Except in the case of Brian, these utterances were not common, and even for Brian, who was the most loquacious of the six children, they constituted only 6 per cent of his descriptions. A number of writers (Bruner, 1975a; Greenfield & Smith, 1976; McNeill, 1970) have placed a heavy emphasis on the holophrastic use of one-word utterances in their theories of the development of linguistic structure. The present findings suggest that holophrases are of limited importance in the development of linguistic structure.

Comparison. Comparisons always involved a child saying that one object was like another object. Only two of the children, Alice and Fiona, made comparisons of this sort. The infrequent occurrence of these utterances is not surprising, as using *like* to relate one object to another requires both a recognition of similarities and a realization that these similarities are not sufficient to give the objects a common label. The majority of Alice's comparisons involved pointing out that people in picture-books were like people she knew (and this followed and replaced the over-extension of personal names to people in picture-books). Fiona's use of *like* was generally to comment that various animals looked like either dogs or horses. However, one example indicates that her recognition of the semantics of 'like' and the logic of class inclusion and exclusion were quite sophisticated. Having called a toy animal *dog* and been told by her mother that it was not a dog, she responded *it looks like a dog, mama*. (Fiona also used *like* in another sense – to indicate that she liked some object. Both uses of *like* were observed for the first time when she was 24 months old. Fiona was the only child to use *like* in the latter way and these utterances were the only observed instances of a child reporting his or her own feelings. These utterances were categorized as Miscellaneous as they are not covered by any existing categories in the present system.)

Denial. Two of the children, Alice and Brian, denied that a proposition could be legitimately aplied to a particular state-of-affairs. Denials were distinguished from Non–existence in that the latter commented on the absence of something whereas the former denied or contradicted some other utterance. Thus, when Alice said *not raining* on turning over a page of a story-book (in which it had been raining in the picture on the previous page) the utterance was categorized as Non-existence, but when she later replied to her mother's comment of . . .*it's easier isn't it?* with *not easy* this was categorized as Denial. When Brian's mother said *poor duck* and Brian replied *no poor duck* the utterance was likewise categorized as Denial. Instances of denial were rare. This is not surprising as denials require some appreciation of the reflexive nature of language (i.e. the potential of language to talk about language). All observed instances of denial had the same linguistic form: they prefaced the proposition being denied with *no* or *not*.

Possession. Utterances indicating possession or ownership by self took one of the following forms: the child said *mine*, or *my X*, or said his or her own name. Possession or ownership by others was generally indicated by saying the other person's name and sometimes adding the name of the object possessed or owned. *Yours* was only used once – by Fiona. Brian and Fiona sometimes indicated possession by others by saying that someone (optional) had something, as for example *got shoes* and *you got lorry*.

Location. The children frequently commented on the location of objects; utterances in this subcategory constituted 23 per cent of all descriptions. Most of these comments included specification of the referent being located; the only locative that was sometimes used as a one-word utterance was *there*. The frequency of use of the different locatives is shown in Table 7. The children occasionally used two locatives together, as for example in *up there* and *in here*; where this occurred the utterance was categorized in Table 7 according to the first locative in the utterance. The subcategory Other includes such locatives as *here, back, upstairs, out, behind*, and *around the back*, all of which were used infrequently.

The most frequently used locative was *there*. Its relative popularity is interesting; *there* is the locative of greatest potential generality as it can be used to refer to any visible location. *In* and *on* were next in frequency of use. It has been claimed (Clark, 1973)

TABLE 7. *Distribution of descriptions in the subcategory Location*

Child	Locative used					
	There	*In*	*On*	*Up*	*Down*	Other
Alice	25	4	10	0	0	3
Brian	128	7	9	10	5	5
Carol	2	1	0	0	0	0
David	5	6	6	2	1	2
Emily	8	1	0	0	0	0
Fiona	34	38	3	6	3	8
Total	202	57	28	18	9	18

that *in* is sometimes treated as if it meant *on* in children's comprehension of these terms. There was no evidence in this study of a similar confusion of meaning in the children's production of these words; when used, *in* and *on* were always used appropriately.

5.3.3 *Information*

Statements that referred beyond the here-and-now were comparatively rare as shown in Table 8. The use of language to refer outside the here-and-now is a complex cognitive and linguistic skill and one which the children were only beginning to master at the time this study ended. Typically utterances categorized as Information consisted of recall of events that had taken place previously. Halliday (1975) has claimed that the use of language to recall events is initially restricted to reporting the events to somebody the child has shared them with. Alice's first observed attempt to use language to inform contradicts the thesis that the experience must be shared in order to be reported.

At 20 months Alice had been looking at a book with her mother when the telephone rang. Alice's mother left to answer the telephone and during her absence Alice continued to look at the book and also began, simultaneously, to blow bubbles with another toy. Alice stopped blowing bubbles after a time but continued to look at the book. When her mother returned Alice turned to her and the following conversation took place:

TABLE 8. *Number of utterances categorized as Information*

Child	Age (months)					
	19	20	21	22	23	24
Alice	0	3	1	—	5	4
Brian	7	1	12	53	21	—
Carol	0	0	0	0	0	9
David	0	0	0	0	1	1
Emily	0	0	0	0	0	4
Fiona	—	0	9	0	2	2

  Alice: *Bubbles.*
 Mother: *Bubbles, yes darling, bubbles.*
    [Alice excitedly replied.]
   A: *Alice.*
   A: *Alice.*
Alice's mother did not understand what Alice was trying to impart but to the author who had been present all the time (filming – and completely ignored by Alice) it was quite evident that Alice was attempting to relate what she had been doing during her mother's absence.

  The majority of utterances in the Information category consisted of recall of events that had taken place previously. Such recall was often prompted by the caretaker questioning the child about something that had happened earlier in the day or even on a previous day. Occasionally instances were observed where the children used language to refer outside the here-and-now for purposes other than recall. The following example illustrates this.

  At 21 months Brian had been eating chocolate. Having finished he asked for more and the following conversation took place:
  Mother: *No, we've finished chocolate now.*
   Brian: *More.*
     [Brian, on receiving no response, changed his tone.]
   B: *Shop.*
   M: *What?*
   B: *Shop Mummy.*
   M: *What?*

B:*Some shop.*
M:*Some more from the shop?*
B: *Yes.*
M:*No.*
[Brian then reverted to requesting more.]

A number of points can be made about this example. As with the example from Alice, Brian's utterences did not semantically express his intended meaning. His meaning, therefore, had to be negotiated with his audience (and it was only in the light of the successful negotiation and Brian's confirmation of his mother's interpretation of his intended meaning that his utterances could be categorized as Information). However, having got his idea across and having had it rejected, Brian reverted to demanding – a display of sensitivity to the appropriateness of different illocutionary forces in the light of changing circumstances.

These findings indicate that by the age of 2 the children were just beginning to exploit the semantic potential of language to refer beyond the here-and-now. Many of the observed instances of this ability consisted of recall of events, sometimes prompted and sometimes not, but some utterances made reference to potential events as in the example above. The development of this ability marks the beginning of what constitutes a major use of language.

5.4 The Exchange categories

These categories include those utterances that accompanied the acts of giving and receiving objects. These activities, in particular giving, were common in the earlier months of the second year. Some of the children frequently exchanged objects with their caretakers and this activity did not appear to have any purpose other than the exchange itself. While the children did not always, or even invariably, accompany the acts of giving and receiving with vocalizations, they sometimes did, and these utterances were coded in the Exchange categories.

Sugarman-Bell (1978) has found a three-step sequence of social-interactive behaviour in preverbal children. First, the children's behaviour is dominated by unitary, repetitive actions directed towards a person or towards an object. This occurs in the first few months of life. Next to appear is differentiated behaviour directed towards a person or object. This occurs from the middle of the first year onwards. Last to appear is integrated person–object activity. This occurs towards the end of the first year. The giving and receiving of objects observed in the early months of the second year is probably one aspect of integrated person–object activity (although there is no direct evidence linking the behaviours reported here with the sequence reported by Sugarman-Bell).

5.4.1 *Giving*

Utterances in this category were those utterances that functionally accompanied the act of giving an object to another person. The data are presented in Figure 12. It can be seen that many of the utterances were not lexicalized, particularly in the earlier months. However, both the verbal and non-verbal behaviour changed over time. More utterances became lexicalized and giving ceased to be a stereotyped repetitive game and only occurred when the child had some particular reason (such as being requested to pass an object) to give. The lexicalized utterances used in giving were subcategorized as follows:

Person: the child uttered the name of the person to whom the object was being given.

Object: the child uttered the name of the object being exchanged.

Here/There: the child said *here* or *there*.

Other: any other lexicalized utterance that accompanied giving.

The distribution of lexicalized utterances is shown in Table 9. A Friedman analysis of variance by ranks did not reveal a consistent preference for the type of utterance used, $\chi_r^2 = 6.35$, $p > 0.05$. Preferences for *here* or *there*, when these utterances were used, were evenly divided for the group as a whole. Of the individual children, Alice had a definite preference for *here* and Brian for *there*. *Thank you* was used by two of the children, Carol and Fiona, to accompany giving. Carol used *thank you* three times during one observation session but the overextension did not appear to survive to any subsequent observations.

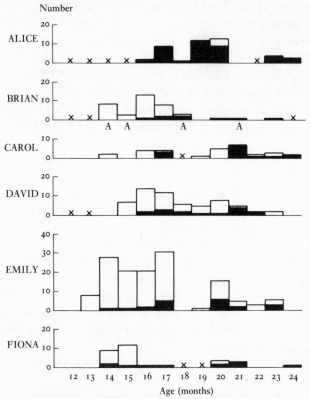

Figure 12. Number of lexicalized and non-lexicalized Giving utterances.
■ Lexicalized utterances; □ non-lexicalized utterances; × no observation at
this age; A average score from two observations

TABLE 9. *Distribution of lexicalized Giving utterances*

| Child | Subcategory | | | |
	Person	Object	*Here/There*	Other
Alice	12	13	12	1
Brian	2	2	7	0
Carol	0	0	11	3
David	3	7	4	1
Emily	3	13	2	2
Fiona	4	2	4	1
Total	24	37	40	8

5.4.2 *Receiving*

Utterances that acknowledged receipt of an object were less common than utterances that accompanied giving. A total of 49 instances was observed of which 17 were lexicalized. Fifteen of the lexicalized utterances were *thank you*. In a small way, the children had begun to learn one of the politeness conventions of language.

5.5 The Personal categories

These categories contain utterances that concerned the child's own participation in activities. Two of the categories, Doing and Determination, concern statements about actions, and two, Refusal and Protest, concern the child's expressed feelings about some activity.

5.5.1 *Doing*

Utterances categorized as Doing were utterances that described some action carried out by the child. These utterances are thus the personal equivalent of the subcategory of Description utterances that described the actions of other people. All Doing utterances were lexicalized by definition. Doing utterances were subcategorized as follows:

Action: the child commented on some action that he or she was performing or had performed by using a verb that described the action.

Location: the child performed some action and commented on either his or her own change in location or the change in location caused to some object. Utterances that specified both the action carried out and the change in location caused were categorized according to the first comment that occurred.

Completion: the child commented on some action that he or she had completed by specifying that the action was completed. (Utterances that occurred after an action had been completed were not necessarily subcategorized as Completion; the criterion is what the utterance describes rather than the temporal occurrence of the utterance.)

TABLE 10. *Distribution of Doing utterances*

Child	Subcategory				
	Action	Location	Completion	Impossible	Other
Alice	4	2	7	1	2
Brian	40	18	72	34	13
Carol	4	2	1	1	0
David	34	6	4	5	2
Emily	5	5	2	2	1
Fiona	25	3	3	18	4
Total	112	36	89	61	22

Impossible: the child commented that he or she could not carry out some action.

Other: any other utterances that described an action performed by the child.

It can be seen from Table 10 that the children frequently described the action they had performed by using a verb that described that particular action. However, 65 per cent of their utterances were not accounted for in this way. Locatives accounted for 11 per cent of their Doing utterances, with *down* and *up* the two most common locatives used in this way. Utterances that specified that the child had completed some activity accounted for 28 per cent of Doing utterances; all of these instances were accounted for by three utterance-types: *there*, *done it*, and *finished*, with *there* accounting for the vast majority (80 per cent). Utterances that described the children's inability to carry out some action accounted for 19 per cent of Doing utterances. The most frequent utterances in this context were *can't* and *no*. Utterances categorized as Other accounted for 11 per cent of Doing utterances with holophrases being the most common type of utterance in this category. However, 11 out of the 14 holophrases were contributed by Brian, who, between 16 and 18 months used *top* both to name markers and to comment on his own action in replacing the top on these. This use of *top* no doubt originated from Brian being asked to *put the top back on* when he had removed the top from the markers.

Although there were similarities in the words the children used to describe their own actions and the actions of others, there were important differences also. The words that were used to specify the action being carried out or the change in location that the child had accomplished were also used to describe the actions of other people, but the words that were used to describe the fact that the child had completed an action or could not carry out some action were never used to describe the actions of others (nor could they readily be so used). Of this latter category, however, both *there* and *no* were extensively used in other speech-acts, where their pragmatic force was quite different from that of Doing utterances.

5.5.2 *Determination*

Utterances in this category were those utterances that referred to some action that the child was about to carry out. All such utterances were lexicalized by definition. There is a similarity between the subcategorization of Determination utterances and Request utterances, in that essentially the same subcategories (with minor modifications of definition) are applicable to both. This is not too surprising in that both types of utterance referred to an activity that the child expected to be carried out. Utterances in the category Determination referred to an activity that the child was about to carry out, whereas utterances in the category Request referred to an activity that the child required somebody else to carry out. Determination utterances were subcategorized as follows:

Person: the child specified the intended recipient of his or her action in advance of carrying out that action.

Recurrence: the child expressed his or her intention to repeat some action by saying, for example, *more* or *again*.

Object: the child specified the object he or she intended to act upon.

Action: the child specified the action he or she intended to carry out.

Conventional Mood: the child used a conventional grammatical means of signalling his or her intention as, for example, by saying *I'm going to...*, *I want...*, or *I need...* prior to acting.

Other: any other utterances categorized as Determination.

Where two subcategories co-occurred in an utterance (as, for

TABLE 11. *Distribution of Determination utterances*

Child	Person	Re-currence	Object	Action	Conventional Mood	Other
Alice	4	7	16	11	2	2
Brian	8	4	33	43	4	10
Carol	0	0	0	0	0	0
David	1	1	6	16	0	0
Emily	1	0	0	1	0	0
Fiona	0	1	9	21	13	0
Total	14	13	64	92	19	12

example, Object and Action) the utterance was categorized on the basis of the first subcategory to occur. As can be seen from Table 11, the children most frequently expressed Determination by specifying either the object that they intended to act upon or by specifying the action that they intended to carry out. These two subcategories alone accounted for 73 per cent of Determination utterances. Of the remaining subcategories Conventional Mood occurred with greatest frequency, although Fiona alone was responsible for the majority of utterances in this subcategory. Fiona's utterances consisted of saying *want* or *want to* in conjunction with a specification of what it was she wanted to do, as, for example, *want do that* or *want to throw it*. Utterances in the Recurrence subcategory consisted primarily of the child saying *more* and utterances in the Person subcategory consisted of the child uttering the name of the person to whom he or she was going to give something as, for example, when Brian said *John* and then picked up a game and brought it to the author. Utterances subcategorized as Other were primarily utterances in which the child specified the location of an intended action as, for example, Brian's uttering *in the lorry* prior to picking up and placing an object in the lorry.

Very few utterances categorized as Determination were observed prior to 18 months. Between 18 months and 2 years four of the children produced quite a wide range of utterances that specified, in some way, their own intentions. In doing so the children displayed their increasing awareness of the semantic potential of language, for these utterances were instances where the children, effectively, were talking to themselves and using language for the purpose of self-guidance.

5.5.3 *Refusal*

Utterances categorized as Refusal were utterances where the child expressed unwillingness to do something in response to the behaviour, either verbal or non-verbal, of another person. Refusals primarily occurred in response to verbal requests by another person. The majority (97 per cent) of refusals were lexicalized and almost invariably consisted of the utterance *no*. Apart from the non-lexicalized utterances the only other exceptions to refusing by saying *no* were Brian's single refusal, at 15 months, of something he had been offered, by saying *bad* and Fiona's two refusals, at 20 months, by saying *don't want it*.

5.5.4 *Protest*

Protests were utterances that expressed the child's displeasure at some state of affairs. Crying was not regarded as protesting as this behaviour does not involve the use of utterances.

Non-lexicalized utterances were frequently used to protest, particularly in the earlier months. Lexicalized protests were mostly a high-pitched *no*. The following utterances were also used to protest. At 17, 18, and 19 months Alice said *mummy* to protest. *Mummy* ceased to be a means of protesting, as it ceased to be a means of requesting (see 5.2.2 above) after 19 months. David (once) and Fiona (twice) also said *mummy* to protest. Brian said *mine* (once) to protest and, on a number of occasions when a favourite object was removed, protested by screaming the object's name.

5.6 The Conversation categories

These categories are different in principle from the other categories. They record how the children's utterances were related to the utterances that were spoken to them. The analysis therefore adopts a different perspective from the preceding analyses, which were concerned with the meaning of the children's individual utterances. This analysis is concerned with how the children's talk can be understood as conversation. The analysis focuses primarily on the types of conversational responses the children made. Some utterances occurred exclusively as conversational responses but there is also an overlap between the Conversation categories and other categories, as responding to an interlocutor's utterance frequently involved communicating something to that interlocutor.

5.6.1 *Imitation*

Imitations accounted for a mean of 19 per cent of conversational responses. They were the least frequent of the three types of conversational response. Figure 13 shows the proportion of conversational responses that were imitations. There were small positive correlations between the frequency of imitation and age, but none was significant. As a conversational strategy, imitations did not show a significant increase during the children's second year.

5.6.2 *Answer*

Adult speech to young children, by comparison with speech to older children and to other adults, has been consistently found to contain a high proportion of questions (see Snow, 1977b; Vorster, 1975 for reviews). In the present study questions constituted on average 26 per cent of adult utterances. The prevalence of questions in adult speech can be viewed as part of the caretaker's attempt to construct a conversational interaction with the child (Snow, 1977a), as questions are a powerful means of turn-allocation (Sacks *et al.*, 1974). In order to determine whether the children were more responsive to questions than to other utterances, the number of answers observed, A_o, was compared to the number of answers expected, A_e, if conversational responses were no more likely after questions than after any other adult utterance. The expected frequency for each child for each month was computed

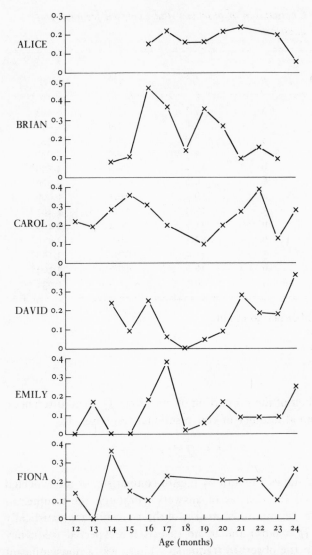

Figure 13. Imitations as a proportion of conversational responses

TABLE 12. *Comparison of observed and expected frequency of Answers to questions*

Age (months)	n	$\overline{A_0}$[a]	$\overline{A_e}$[a]	t[b]
12	3	7.1	5.9	2.495
13	3	6.8	4.9	1.072
14	5	8.9	5.4	1.457
15	5	4.7	2.6	2.026
16	6	10.4	6.0	4.599**
17	6	6.9	4.9	3.288*
18	4	16.5	10.1	1.606
19	5	17.4	10.5	2.461*
20	6	31.6	19.4	2.405*
21	6	42.4	26.6	2.434*
22	5	41.4	26.1	3.182*
23	6	30.9	18.2	3.304*
24	5	46.5	31.6	1.634

[a] Mean number per 30 minutes.
[b] One-tailed.
  * $p < 0.05$.
 ** $p < 0.01$.

as the product of the proportion of questions, Q, to all utterances, U, by the total number of conversational responses, C.

$$A_e = Q/U \times C$$

Table 12 shows a month by month comparison of the expected and observed frequencies of answers. Although the number of observations per month is small, 7 of the 13 results are statistically significant ($p < 0.05$) and in no case is the expected frequency greater than the observed frequency. There was a nonsignificant correlation between the ratio of observed to expected frequency of answers and age, $r = 0.46$, $p > 0.05$. Analysis on a child by child basis revealed that in all cases answers occurred with significantly greater than expected frequency ($p < 0.05$ in all cases).

On what basis were questions selectively identified as requiring a response by the children? The present study cannot answer this definitively. Both surface structure syntax and prosody are obvious candidate cues. Questions generally have a distinct grammatical form and frequently end with a rising intonation, although they are not unique in this latter respect. Garnica (1977) has shown that speech to 2-year-old children frequently ends in rising intonation even if the utterance is a statement or an imperative. However, other factors such as pitch-level may help to discriminate the rising intonation of a question from that of other speech-acts. Schafer (1922) and Lewis (1936) have both reported non-verbal responses (orientation towards an object) to utterances that had the intonation but not the native lexical form of a question. However, an experimental attempt to produce non-verbal responses to question intonation alone failed to find a significant effect (Macnamara, 1977), although this may have been due to the rather unusual situations involved in the experiment. The factors that selectively identified questions as requiring a conversational response must, for the moment, remain uncertain.

The proportion of lexicalized answers at each observation is shown in Figure 14. In the earlier months most of the children's responses to questions consisted of non-lexicalized utterances. There was no indication in the earlier months, either from their answers or from their non-verbal behaviour, that the children had any understanding of the questions to which they responded. Thus, the activity of participating in conversation developed before the children had any literal understanding of what the conversation was about. Their responses might be called 'phatic', to borrow Malinowski's (1923) term, in that they appeared to occur for the sake of the interaction itself. The children's lexicalized answers were subcategorized as follows:

Statement: the child's answer either named an object or described some attribute or action of an object or event that the child had been asked about.

Regulation: the child's answer was an attempt to regulate the behaviour of his or her interlocutor by requesting, or drawing attention to, some object, action or event.

Yes: the child answered *yes* to a question.

No: the child answered *no* to a question.

Other: any other utterance spoken by the child in answer to a question.

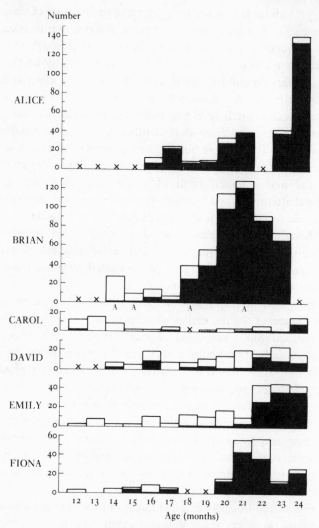

Figure 14. Number of lexicalized and non-lexicalized Answers.
For key see Figure 12

It can be seen from Table 13 that statements were the most common type of lexicalized answer. The large number of answers that consisted of statements reflects the fact that the children were frequently encouraged to name and describe the objects and events of their immediate environment. It was a notable feature of

TABLE 13. *Distribution of lexicalized Answers*

Child	Statement	Regulation	*Yes*	*No*	Other
			Subcategory		
Alice	130 (0.40)	16 (0.05)	59 (0.18)	44 (0.14)	45 (0.14)
Brian	190 (0.24)	53 (0.07)	176 (0.23)	106 (0.14)	79 (0.06)
Carol	5 (0.07)	0 (0)	4 (0.05)	3 (0.04)	5 (0.07)
David	27 (0.17)	5 (0.03)	4 (0.03)	4 (0.03)	16 (0.10)
Emily	82 (0.38)	7 (0.03)	3 (0.01)	4 (0.02)	12 (0.06)
Fiona	114 (0.57)	3 (0.01)	4 (0.02)	6 (0.03)	11 (0.05)
Total	548	84	250	167	168

Note. Numbers in parentheses are the proportions of Answers represented by the preceding numbers. Non-lexicalized Answers account for the residual proportions.

questions that attempted to elicit statements that the statement required was almost always a statement about a visible object or event. Only towards the end of the second year did some of the caretakers' questions begin to request statements that went beyond the here-and-now, an adjustment no doubt motivated by the children's increasing linguistic proficiency. Question–answer exchanges about the here-and-now can be seen as a means whereby the dyads, to a greater or lesser extent, focused on just those aspects of linguistic structure – names and descriptions – that the children were currently mastering. By initiating such exchanges the caretakers were encouraging and enabling the children to discover the relationship between their cognitive ordering of the environment and the lexicon and linguistic structure necessary to express this ordering in speech.

Responses that consisted of either *yes* or *no* were frequent in the cases of Alice and Brian only. Although *yes* and *no* were used to respond to Yes–No questions, these utterances were also used at times to fulfil the social requirement of taking a conversational turn to other question-types when the children had clearly lost the semantic drift of the conversation. In these cases it seemed that the demand of making some response was paramount while the meaning of the response was secondary. This phenomenon was not

confined to the initial stages of using these words as the examples
below illustrate.

At 23 months the following conversation took place between
Alice and her mother:

>Mother: *Look Alice, look what I've got.*
>
>*Look, look.*
>
>*Mike's Christmas present, isn't it?*
>
>*What is it?*
>
>Alice: (points) *That.*
>
>M: *What is it?*
>
>*What is it in here?*
>
>A: *Yes.*
>
>M: *What is it?*
>
>A: (nods her head) *Yes.*

In this incident the mother produced a box that contained a present
for Alice's cousin, Mike. However, Alice was neither familiar with
the object nor, in all probability, with the concept of Christmas
presents, so she failed to provide the required description of the
box. She did recognize that a response was required to her mother's
question and so she provided one, identifying the object as *that*.
At this stage of her development Alice called every object whose
name she did not know *that*. The context in which this was most
frequently observed to occur was book reading. Her mother would
ask Alice *what's that?* and Alice would respond with an emphatic
that. Her mother would then typically name the object. Here the
mother did not do this, perhaps because she had already named
the object. Alice could not carry the conversation about the name
of the object any further on this occasion and so she resorted to
providing a response of assent on being further asked *what is it?*
The question was not itself unintelligible to her; it was the context
in which the question occurred which defeated her.

At 21 months the following conversation took place between
Brian and his father immediately after his mother had gone
shopping:

>Father: *Where's she going?*
>
>Brian: *Gone.*
>
>F: *What?*
>
>B: *Mummy buy sweetie.*
>
>[Father did not hear this utterance clearly.]

> F: *Mummy's what?*
> B: *Eh Mummy buy sweetie.*
> F: *Bake city?*
>   *Big city?*
> B: *Yes.*
> F: *Ah she's going to the big city is she?*
> B: *Yes.*
> F: *What's she going to buy?*
>   [Brian's father, having asked this question, suddenly understood Brian's earlier utterance.]
> F: *Oh she buys sweeties.*
> B: *Ye-es.*

In this conversation Brian's two initial uses of *yes* differed from his final *yes*. The first two were uttered in a somewhat perfunctory manner in response to his father's attempt to clarify the initial utterance. *No* would have been a more appropriate response but Brian had not yet learnt the skill of correcting the semantic content of another person's utterance, so there was therefore no particular motivation to use *no* in preference to *yes*. The last *yes* was altogether different however. The conversation had now returned to the topic Brian had introduced and the emphatic and drawn out *ye-es* conveyed his feeling of "now you've got it".

Answers categorized as Regulation did not occur with a high frequency and the residual category consisted of both a variety of speech-acts occurring with low frequency and a variety of words whose meaning, pragmatically or semantically, was uncertain but which provided the obligatory response to a question.

5.6.3 *Follow-on*

Utterances in this category were those conversational responses that were neither imitations nor answers. As with answers, non-lexicalized follow-ons were more common in the earlier months of the second year, as can be seen in Figure 15. It is not clear in the case of follow-ons what the initial basis of conversational participation was. The children responded to a wide variety of parental utterances with a follow-on but no linguistic or paralinguistic features seemed to be shared by these utterances. The simplest explanation is that the children were generally responsive to talk

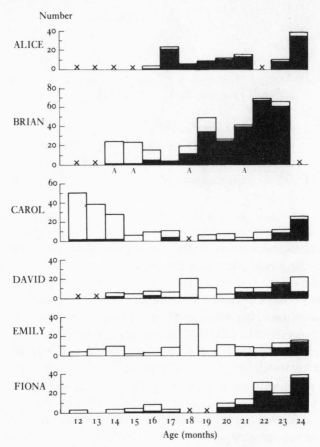

Figure 15. Number of lexicalized and non-lexicalized Follow-ons.
For key see Figure 12

addressed to them but when the talk took the form of a question
the probability of responding increased. Lexicalized follow-ons
were divided into the same subcategories as lexicalized answers.
The results are shown in Table 14.

Overall, statements were still the most frequent type of response
although their relative frequency as follow-ons was considerably
less than as questions (26 per cent as against 45 per cent), and one
child, Fiona, contributed over 40 per cent of the statements in this
category. It has already been shown that statements occurred

TABLE 14. *Distribution of lexicalized Follow-ons*

Child	Statement	Regulation	*Yes*	*No*	Other
			Subcategory		
Alice	27 (0.22)	9 (0.07)	7 (0.06)	36 (0.30)	28 (0.23)
Brian	46 (0.10)	13 (0.29)	96 (0.21)	91 (0.20)	61 (0.13)
Carol	1 (0.00)	4 (0.02)	10 (0.05)	14 (0.07)	19 (0.09)
David	12 (0.09)	6 (0.05)	1 (0.01)	6 (0.05)	19 (0.15)
Emily	7 (0.05)	4 (0.03)	0 (0)	1 (0.01)	18 (0.13)
Fiona	71 (0.50)	3 (0.02)	0 (0)	13 (0.09)	10 (0.70)
Total	164	39	114	161	155

Note. Numbers in parentheses are the proportions of Follow-ons represented by the preceding numbers. Non-lexicalized Follow-ons account for the residual proportions.

significantly more often than chance following a question (and this of course reflects the type of questions that caretakers asked the children). Comparison of Tables 13 and 14 reveals that the absolute number of statements following questions was greater, in all cases, than the number following all other utterance-types, and that over three times as many statements occurred in response to questions as in response to other utterance-types. It is obviously the case that naming and describing within a conversation are best facilitated by question–answer exchanges.

Utterances that consisted of *yes* and *no* accounted for an overall 43 per cent of lexicalized follow-ons. The most common use of *no* was to refuse to carry out a request or a suggestion made by the caretaker, as in the following example.

Mother: *Come and have a sleep.*
Alice: *No.*
M: *Come and have a little sleep.*
A: *No.*

The most common uses of *yes* can best be illustrated by example.

Mother: *You're a good girl.*
Carol: *Yes yes.*
Mother: *Gone, washing the plates upstairs.*

      Brian: *Yes.*

        M: *Yes, giving the plates a wash.*

        B: *Yes.*

In these latter examples it is not obvious whether the children were responding simply to the fact that they had been spoken to or whether they were, in addition, giving their assent to the proposition expressed. However, towards the end of their second year it became obvious, in some cases, that the children were using *yes* and *no* to either affirm or contradict the specific semantic content of their interlocutor's utterance. The subtle difference is reflected in the two following examples.

At 22 months Brian and his mother were playing with a train set. Brian picked up an engine and the following exchange took place.

      Brian: *I find it.*

    Mother: *That's the engine.*

        B: *No.*

        M: *Yes.*

        B: *No.*

        M: *It is.*

        B: *No.*

        M: *That's the engine.*

        B: *Yes.*

        M: *And the others are carriages.*

        B: *Yes.*

In this exchange there was a real dispute over the name of the object that Brian had picked up. Brian initially denied his mother's assertion that the object was an engine but finally came round to accepting that it was.

At 24 months Alice and her mother were blowing up balloons for the Christmas tree. Alice's mother had just inflated a large balloon. Alice picked up a balloon that was only partially inflated, and the following exchange took place.

      Alice: *Baby.*

    Mother: *A baby one.*

        A: *Yes.*

        M: (holding up the large balloon) *What's this one?*

        A: *That's mummy.*

M: *A mummy one.*

A: (nodding her head) *Yes.*

In this exchange Alice confirmed her mother's interpretation of the metaphoric use of *baby*, initially by her response of *yes*, then further by her appropriate use of the contrast "mummy–baby" when asked *what's this one?*, and finally she confirmed the mother's expansion of this utterance with another *yes*.

Such instances as those reported above were comparatively rare, but they show the degree of conversational sophistication that the children were capable of by the age of 2, despite the fact that this sophistication was often revealed in utterances only one word long.

5.6.4 *Question*

So far the discussion of conversation has concentrated on the responses that the children made to another person's utterances. In conversation one participant must initiate the dialogue. The children's utterances frequently had the effect of initiating a conversation but it was impossible to determine, more often than not, whether they had so intended. Although initiations, whether intentional or not, are of considerable interest in the study of dyads, the discussion here will be restricted to the only clear case of the intentional initiation of conversation by the children: questions. Table 15 reveals that questions occurred comparatively rarely and that it was only towards the latter part of their second year that the children began to ask questions. Questions were subcategorized as shown in Table 16. It can be seen that *where* and *what* questions were the most frequent type: together they accounted for 66 per cent of all questions. The paradigmatic uses of *where* and *what* were to ask for the location of an object and the name of an object. Thus, the types of information the children elicited constituted ways of describing their immediate environment. *Where* and *what* questions were also the only questions that occurred as one-word utterances. Yes–No questions occurred with a lower frequency than *where* and *what* questions although these former questions apparently become the most common type of question used by children between 2 and 5 years old (Smith, 1933; Tyack & Ingram, 1977). In common with other studies (Brown, 1973; Tyack & Ingram, 1977) it was found

TABLE 15. *Number of Questions*

Child	Age (months)				
	20	21	22	23	24
Alice	2	4	–	6	12
Brian[a]	1	0	8	31	–
Carol	0	0	0	1	1
David	0	0	0	0	1
Emily	0	0	0	2	2
Fiona	8	1	3	4	21
Mean	1.8	0.8	1.8	7.3	6.2

[a] Brian also asked one question at 16 months.

TABLE 16. *Number of each question-type*

Child	Wh-					Yes–No	
	Where	*What*	*Who*	*How*	*Why*	Normal	Tag
Alice	2	16	0	0	0	6	0
Brian	28	4	0	3	1	5	0
Carol	1	1	0	0	0	0	0
David	1	0	0	0	0	0	0
Emily	0	4	0	0	0	0	0
Fiona	9	6	3	0	2	8	9
Total	41	31	3	3	3	19	9

that Yes–No questions were not always syntactically well-formed but were nevertheless clearly recognizable on intonational criteria.

The remainder of the question-types, *who, how,* and *why* were not common. Only Fiona asked *who* questions and only three were asked in all, one at 23 months and two at 24 months. Brian asked three *how* questions at 23 months and one *why* question at 22 months, and Fiona asked two *why* questions at 24 months.

Thus, by the end of their second year, the children had begun to use language to request that specific pieces of information be provided by an interlocutor, although the present study only documents its very earliest stages. In learning this they were beginning to discover that language can be used to select and control the information received and thus they were beginning to discover the potential of language as a means of learning, in addition to its existing uses as a means of communication.

5.7 The Miscellaneous category

Utterances categorized as Miscellaneous constituted 5 per cent of all utterances, and the only child with a higher than average percentage of Miscellaneous utterances was David with 9 per cent. Most of the Miscellaneous utterances were either noises, or words that appeared to be uttered for their own sake, or singing. The only utterances categorized as Miscellaneous because they were of a degree of sophistication not generally evidenced in the group as a whole were utterances made by Fiona at the age of 24 months. Some of these utterances were statements about the child's feelings – for example, *Fiona like this elephant* – something none of the other children was observed to express by making a statement. Other utterances stated various courses of action that could be taken by one or other of her toys in a game as, for example, *he can have a cup of tea*, or the two successive utterances *he can have another bath*, *if he want to*.

5.8 Summary of the children's progress

Alice. Alice was first observed at 16 months and even at this age the majority of her utterances were lexicalized, the only child in the sample for whom this was true before 18 months. During the early observations the pragmatic and conversational uses of language were evident, but Naming was the only type of statement observed. Although she was intelligible, her initial range of utterances was nevertheless limited: *mummy* was an all-purpose pragmatic utterance and *no* was used for both pragmatic and conversational purposes. At 17 months *more* was introduced as an additional means of requesting, and object names were also frequently used to request on this and subsequent occasions. This pattern, with some extension of the vocabulary used, continued until 19 months. At this age there was an increase in naming and Alice's mother reported at this time that Alice "loved naming things". Descriptions and structured utterances were first common in Alice's speech at 20 months. From this age onwards *mummy* ceased to be an all-purpose pragmatic utterance and was subsequently only used to name mothers in picture-books or as a vocative. Questions were first observed at 20 months also. Apart from the initiation of conversation by asking questions, Alice also began to add personal names as address terms to some of her statements, thus passing on an obligatory conversational turn to her interlocutor. This strategy was not, however, common in her case.

Brian. At 14 months, when first observed, Brian was capable of extensive pragmatic communication although most of his utterances were not lexicalized. His most consistent lexicalized utterances on the early observations were *mama* and *dada*, which he always used either to request, to direct attention, or to call the person in question. Although there was no evidence, at this stage, that these words were names for Brian's mother and father, they were nevertheless always used to interact with the appropriate person. Brian had other means of requesting and directing attention. Up to the age of 17 months he frequently requested by uttering *eheheh* with a high pitch and rising intonation. From 18 months onwards names were commonly used to request. From 15 months onwards the most common method of directing attention was to alternate between *luh* (probably an attempt at *look*) and *uh*. *Luh* was used at 15 months, but at 16 months the utterances that directed attention were much less consistent in form, although all were variations on the theme of *uh*. By 17 months *look* was definitely established. In the early months *no* was also a common utterance, being used to refuse, to protest, and as a conversational response. At 18 months names, descriptions, and structured utterances became common in Brian's speech. For the first time, at this age, more than 50 per cent of Brian's utterances were lexicalized and the proportion had risen to 95 per cent during the last three observations. Also at 18 months personal names were added to utterances as address terms on a few occasions. This strategy was common by 19 months and very frequent from 20 months onwards.

Questions were observed on the last two observations at 22 and 23 months. Brian was probably the child most sensitive to turn-taking in conversation. He invariably responded to an utterance addressed to him (frequently with *yes* or *no*, when it was obvious that he had not understood the semantic content of the utterance) and from 18 months onwards he increasingly ensured turn-allocation by providing his own utterance with an address.

Carol. The data for Carol are quite puzzling. She was extremely vocal during the first three observations at 12, 13 and 14 months although most of her utterances were lexically unintelligible. The most striking thing about these utterances, however, was that a high proportion constituted conversational responses. Imitations were common, but answers and follow-ons were even more common. However, at 15 months the proportion of conversational responses was less than half any previous proportion, and her utterance rate had also decreased. Thereafter her utterance rate dropped to the point where she was consistently the least vocal child, and she was also one of the slowest in learning language. During the period from 12 to 15 months one important change was noticed in Carol's speech. Her utterances changed gradually towards a high-pitched and communicatively unintelligible babble. This was not observed at all at 12 months, had begun at 13 months although it still occurred in a minority of utterances, was more common at 14 months, and prevalent at 15 months when the utterance rate had dropped. This continued to characterize Carol's utterances until the end of the study. Her low utterance rate from 15 months onwards was matched by a low utterance rate from her mother and so, effectively, very little communication took place. The interactions between Carol and her mother were among the least structured interactions observed as there was no evident favourite game or pastime. Pedagogic attempts by Carol's mother were noticeably absent; the mother only joined in activities at Carol's insistence and she rarely made any attempt to prolong these activities. Lexicalized utterances were not common in Carol's speech. At 13 and 14 months *mama* was used to request but was not so used again till the last observation at 2 years. *Mama* was occasionally used as a vocative in the intervening period. From 17 months onwards *no* was sometimes used to refuse and to protest.

Look was used as a means of directing attention at 21 months. Naming was occasionally observed from 20 months onwards but never occurred with a high frequency. A number of developments were evident on the last observation. Lexicalized utterances constituted more than 50 per cent of Carol's speech for the first time. Descriptions were observed with some frequency, as were structured utterances, and the majority of request utterances were lexicalized for the first time.

David. David was the most active of the children in that he rarely stayed in one place for very long; games were frequently punctuated by a foray to another part of the room. During the first three observations at 14, 15 and 16 months there were many instances of onomatopoeia during the course of games with farm animals. The sounds were usually appropriate to the animals concerned, but the utterances did not appear to be attempts to name the animals as they usually had a sing-song intonation. David did sometimes name the animals appropriately and these utterances differed in pitch from the onomatopoeic utterances, further suggesting that the latter were not labels. Lexicalized requests were first prominent at 18 months with *more* and some object names being used to request. Both types of utterance persisted thereafter but structured utterances were rarely used to request until 24 months. However, structured utterances were common as descriptions from 21 months onwards. At 22 months, for the first time, more than 50 per cent of David's utterances were lexicalized. David's participation in conversation was not extensive. Only 7 per cent of his statements were uttered in response to questions compared with the group mean of 18 per cent. The relation between questions from David's mother and answers from David was different from any of the other dyads observed. Whereas in all the other dyads there was a large and significant positive correlation between questions and answers, the correlation in David's case was only 0.32 and it was not significant. There was a significant negative correlation ($r = -0.62$, $p < 0.05$) between age and the relative frequency of maternal questions. This was the only dyad for whom this pattern was observed. Obviously question–answer sequences were not a successful conversational strategy for David and his mother. Part of the reason for this was, no doubt, the difficulty of holding a conversation with a child so frequently in motion.

Emily. Emily was one of the more taciturn children; only Carol had a lower mean utterance rate. In the early months of observation Emily frequently played a game that consisted of giving objects, one after the other, to her mother. Many of these exchanges were accompanied by a non-lexicalized Giving utterance. Requests and conversational responses were also evident in the first part of the second year although none of these utterances was lexicalized. From 19 months onwards Emily enjoyed looking at picture-books with her mother. Initially her participation was to point to pictures and utter *dah* to call attention to what she was pointing to. At 22 months, however, the utterance used to direct attention changed to *look* and, at the same time, naming the objects in the book began although, at this age, associating the object with a familiar person was more common than labelling. This is illustrated in the following example where mother and child were looking at a picture-book.

    Mother: *What are they?*
    Emily: *Dada.*
        M: *Daddy's got one yes, what are they?*
        [no response from Emily.]

During the remaining observations at 23 and 24 months labelling continued to increase. At 23 months, for the first time, structured utterances occurred with some frequency and more than 50 per cent of Emily's utterances were lexicalized. Descriptions were evident at 24 months although most descriptions were still one-word utterances.

Fiona. Fiona was the most loquacious of the girls. (It is an odd fact that the mean utterance rate for both boys is higher than that for any of the girls.) Most of the early observations were uneventful, however, in that relatively little communication took place between Fiona and her mother. It is probable that this was due to the presence of an observer and this is the one case where it was felt that what was being observed initially was atypical of the mother–child interaction. However, by 16 months Fiona exhibited a wide range of communicative utterances, some of which were lexicalized. *Look* was used to direct attention, *mama* and *again* were used to request, *there* was used to indicate location, and both *more* and *again* were used to express Fiona's own intention to repeat some action. At 17 months naming was evident with some frequency. The proportion of lexicalized utterances increased dramatically from 18 per cent at 16 months to 48 per cent at 17 months. By the next observation, which did not take place till 20 months, both descriptions and structured utterances were common and became extensive in the following months. Fiona began to add personal names to her own utterances as address terms at 22 months. This strategy of turn-allocation was particularly frequent at 23 months but much less so at 2 years. She began to ask questions at 20 months and by 2 years had mastered *where*, *what*, *who*, *why*, and Yes–No questions. During the last observation at 2 years she also began to express in language her own preferences by saying whether or not she liked particular toys. She was the only child observed to do this.

6

Learning to talk

6.0 The development of communication

Language development takes place in a context of social interaction between a child and his or her caretakers. The central argument of this book is that language development is the product of intentional communication between a child and other people. The intention to communicate is not a "primitive" with which the child is innately endowed, but it may be a primitive of the child–caretaker dyad. From the earliest months of life a child's caretaker will systematically respond to the child's utterances as if these utterances were intentional, and the child will thus come to learn that there are contingent relations between his or her own utterances and the behaviour of other people. By learning these contingent relations and by learning to behave in order to produce the contingency the child learns to behave intentionally. The results presented here indicate that communicative intentions are evident before words are learnt. This suggests that language development proceeds from intention to convention. It is primarily this process that I want to discuss further in this chapter.

The earliest communicative behaviours the children learnt were the paradigmatically pragmatic ones of requesting, directing attention, giving, and protesting. The complete ontogenesis of these speech-acts cannot be traced here as these communicative behaviours were present from the beginning of this study at 12 months. But, for requesting, the research of Bates *et al.* (1975) and of Sugarman-Bell (1978) suggests that children initially learn to request interaction with other people, later learning to request other people to act as intermediaries in pursuit of actions on objects. By the beginning of their second year the children in this study could request and communicate certain other pragmatic intentions to another person. Thus, the children could produce utterances devoid of semantic content, which, in context, communicated their intentions.

When the children came to learn to use words for pragmatic acts of communication it was clear that at least some of the words used by them were not comparable to their homonymic equivalents in the adult language, in that these words were functionally restricted to certain speech-acts or certain types of speech-acts. For most of the children personal names were the most useful all-purpose pragmatic utterance, but specific utterances also had their uses in particular cases: *look* to direct attention, *more* to request recurrence, *here* and *there* to accompany the giving of an object, and *no* to refuse and protest. In addition some object and action words were used by most of the children for pragmatic communication about particular objects and actions. Even this limited range of utterances forms a successful communication system and one with a number of lexical conventions. But the route to a structured language does not lie in these developments. That route lies through the development of naming.

Up to a point the development of naming can be understood in essentially the same framework as the development of the pragmatic speech-acts discussed above. The child does not initially possess an intention of using language to name objects but nevertheless his or her utterances in certain situations are treated as if they were attempts at naming, whether these utterances consist of a word or not (Ninio & Bruner, 1978). These situations have the characteristics of a ritual in that some joint activity is repeatedly carried out with a small range of familiar objects. The joint activity frequently concerns looking at picture-books with at least one partner naming the objects pictured. Certain contingent relations attend the advances the child makes in his or her participation, notably reinforcement for "appropriate" responses and a raising of the criterion of participation necessary for further reinforcement. In such situations the child learns to play the game by uttering names at appropriate points in the ritual. But uttering names does not yet constitute naming. The concept of naming must also be acquired, for naming involves not just an association between word and object within the context of a ritual encounter but an understanding of a particular type of conceptual relationship between language and the world. That understanding develops as a result of insight on the child's part that the behaviour in which he or she has been engaging during these ritual encounters is one of naming. Naming marks the beginning of the use of language to talk about the world. It precedes the use of words to describe attributes and actions but these shortly follow as a direct result of naming. If there are words that refer to objects then there can be words that refer to attributes, actions, and other salient aspects of the world. The development of language structure follows from this, for these different words can be combined to describe the different elements of some perceived event. The development of language structure is not restricted in its application to making statements about the world, although structure is most evident and most pervasive in statements. It must be remembered too that the child's achievements do not occur in splendid isolation from a communicating environment. During the course of these developments children are being continually encouraged to extend their abilities to talk. Once they have learnt to describe the environment they are encouraged to extend these descriptions beyond the here-and-now. The use of language to inform was the last use of statements to develop and it was only beginning at the time this study ended. At the same time the children were also beginning to ask questions to elicit the types of information they wished to be provided with.

Language is a system that exhibits structure but there is also a large range of social conventions that must be mastered to ensure felicitous communication. From the earliest months of this study it was obvious that the children were simultaneously mastering the structural and social conventions of language. At the beginning of their second year they were responsive to the utterances of others, especially if these utterances were questions. These initial conversational responses were non-lexicalized utterances. Later conversations were frequently built around naming and describing the world. In addition to this, two of the children frequently responded to another's utterance with *yes* and *no*. These utterances were sometimes flagrantly inappropriate from the adult point of view but they nevertheless served to accomplish the task of taking a turn. The nuances of appropriateness were gradually mastered to the point where, at the end of the second year, these children could affirm or contradict the propositional content of another's utterance. A further conversational strategy that was mastered by three of the children was the addition of an address term as a means of securing turn-allocation following the child's own utterance.

The children had learnt a wide variety of words by the time they were 2 years old but their mastery of *there* and *no* is worth particular comment in view of the disparate uses to which these words were put. *There* was commonly used to describe the location of objects. It was by far the most frequent locative used for this purpose. *There* is a deictic term that can be used to specify any location in interpersonal space apart from the speaker's immediate personal space. Its frequency of use demonstrates that the children were aware of its almost all-purpose appropriateness as a locative. *There* was also used to accompany the exchange of objects and to signal the completion of an action by the child. There was no particular order in which *there* was incorporated into these different types of utterance; often the three uses of *there* all occurred for the first time during the same observation.

The initial uses of *no* were to refuse to carry out some action requested by another person, to protest at some intrusion by another person, to forbid another person to carry out some action, and to make a conversational response. Not all of the children used *no* in all of these ways but, for those who did, these uses were first observed within one month of each other. The next observed use of *no* was in combination with other words, to comment on the absence of additional instances of something (e.g. *no more*), or to comment on the absence of some expected state (e.g. *no work*). At this time a further use of *no* as a one-word utterance was observed: to comment that the child had failed to carry out some action that he or she had attempted to carry out. The final observed use of *no* was its use in conversation to deny or contradict a proposition expressed by another person. These uses of *no* can be compared to the uses of negation reported by Bloom (1970). She distinguished three categories of Negation: Rejection, Non-existence, and Denial which emerged in that order in the speech of the children she studied. The present findings confirm this order of emergence but add the further uses of *no* as a conversational response and as a description of one's own failure to carry out an action.

6.1 Meaning as intending

In 1.1 I introduced Grice's theory of meaning. In Grice's theory meaning is explained in terms of the utterer's intentions. In 1.1 and 1.2 I tried to show how intentional communication might develop, and the remainder of this book has been concerned with how a conventional system develops from intentional communication. If my programme has been successful it should bring us, via Gricean intentions, to conventional communication. Let us first reconsider Gricean intentions and then turn to conventional communication. Grice's (1957) account was specifically formulated to deal with statements and imperatives. His original account was:

Statements:

If S utters X thereby meaning that P, S utters X intending

  (i) that some audience A should come to believe P,

 (ii) that A should be aware of intention (i), and

(iii) that the awareness mentioned in (ii) should be part of A's reason for believing P.

Imperatives:

If S utters X thereby meaning that A is to do Y, S utters X intending

  (i) that A should do Y,

 (ii) that A should be aware of intention (i), and

(iii) that the awareness mentioned in (ii) should be part of A's reason for doing Y.

That was the account of imperatives I adopted in 1.1, but the account of statements was amended, following Schiffer (1972), to read:

  If S utters X thereby meaning that P, S utters X intending

  (i) that some audience A should come to have the activated belief that P,

 (ii) that A should be aware of intention (i), and

(iii) that the awareness mentioned in (ii) should be part of A's reason for having the activated belief that P.

That amendment covers cases where the audience already knows the information that the speaker's utterance conveys and the speaker knows that the audience knows this, but the speaker wishes to remind the audience, draw the information to their attention, and so on. But that 'and so on' is problematic. Just how many different intentions are possible in making statements? The intention to remind an audience that P is not quite the same as the intention to induce belief in an audience that P, which is not quite the same as the intention to inform the audience that the speaker believes that P. Yet, it seems undeniable that a statement may be legitimately made with any of these intentions. I think that the problem here lies in an assumption in Grice's formulation that none of the proposed revisions of that formulation has adequately tackled: that there is a one-to-one relation between intention-types and utterance-types. That assumption seems to work for imperatives but it seems to be false for statements. Schiffer's (1972) proposed revision broadens the intention-type but if the intentional specification is to be sufficiently broad to cover all cases it is in danger of losing internal coherency. In view of this it may be better to dispense with the attempt to formulate a sufficiently broad intention-type to cover all these cases and regard statements as having a family of possible intentions, one of which will be operative on a particular occasion of use. With that in mind I propose that the intentional conditions for statements be formulated as follows:

If S utters X thereby meaning that P, S utters X intending
  (i) that some audience A should come to have some particular belief Y concerning P,
 (ii) that A should be aware of intention (i), and
(iii) that the awareness mentioned in (ii) should be part of A's reason for having the particular belief Y.

The variable Y is some member of the family of beliefs that one can legitimately induce by making statements and this family is a mirror image of the family of intentions that S can legitimately have in making a statement. Family membership I regard as a matter for empirical investigation. The advantage of this formulation as applied to language development is that it allows the development of different types of intentions that attend the uttering of statements to be studied. It has already been shown that statements that convey information about the here-and-now are developmentally prior to statements that convey information that go beyond the here-and-now. The former types of utterance seem to be cases where the speaker's intention is to inform the audience that the speaker believes the proposition asserted, and the latter types of utterance seem to be cases where the speaker wishes to induce in the audience the belief that the proposition is true. (This applies to the case of spontaneous utterances.)

In Grice's theory, to understand meaning one has to understand intentions. But intentions are not observable, they are made manifest in the speaker's behaviour. One way of making an intention manifest is through the conventional meaning of an utterance. The utterance must adequately convey the intention; a speaker cannot hope to make an intention clear unless he or she adopts some conventional means of expressing that intention; otherwise the road to Babble is paved with good intentions (Ziff, 1967: 5). The question for a developmental account of language is this: what are the conventions of intentional communication that children learn? I have tried to show the ways in which various conventions are learnt so that a formative semantic system has begun to operate by the age of 2 years. But I do not wish to imply that the conventions of communication after this point rest entirely on the semantic nature of language. That position will not do because there is no one-to-one connection between what a speaker says and what he or she means (between the mood of an utterance and the illocutionary force of the utterance). I believe that an adequate theory of language development must continue to trace not only the structural developments in the child's language but also the development and refinement of the communicative potential of different types of linguistic structure. The sophistication of adult speech, where what is implied is often more important than what is said, is a long way off, and it is surely a developmental story worth the telling.

References (and citation index)

Note. Page references for citations in the text are given in square brackets.

Argyle, M. & Cook, M. (1976). *Gaze and mutual gaze.* Cambridge: Cambridge University Press. [58]

Austin, J. (1962). *How to do things with words.* Oxford: Oxford University Press. [24–5, 81]

Bates, E. (1976). *Language and context.* New York: Academic Press. [54]

Bates, E., Camaioni, L. & Volterra, V. (1975). The acquisition of performatives prior to speech. *Merrill–Palmer Quarterly, 21,* 205–26. [24, 27–30, 36, 37, 45, 54, 91, 145]

Bateson, M. C. (1971). Speech communication: the interpersonal context of infant vocalization. *Quarterly Progress Reports of the Research Laboratory of Electronics* (M.I.T.), *100,* 170–6. [57, 65]

Beattie, G. (1978a). Floor apportionment and gaze in conversational dyads. *British Journal of Social and Clinical Psychology, 17,* 7–15. [61, 64]

Beattie, G. (1978b). Sequential temporal patterns of speech and gaze in dialogue. *Semiotica, 23,* 29–52. [58, 64]

Bennett, J. (1976). *Linguistic behaviour.* Cambridge: Cambridge University Press. [4, 6–7]

Bloom, L. (1970). *Language development: form and function in emerging grammars.* Cambridge, Mass.: M.I.T. Press. [12, 17, 148]

Bloom, L. (1973). *One word at a time.* The Hague: Mouton. [15–16, 19–22, 36, 37, 41, 50, 113–14]

Bloom, L., Lightbown, P. & Hood, L. (1975). Structure and variation in child language. *Monographs of the Society for Research in Child Development, 40* (2, serial no. 160). [37]

Bloom, L., Rocissano, L. & Hood, L. (1976). Adult–child discourse: developmental interaction between information processing and linguistic knowledge. *Cognitive Psychology, 8,* 521–52. [67]

Bower, T. (1974). *Development in infancy.* San Francisco: Freeman. [42]

Braine, M. (1963). The ontogeny of English phrase structure: the first phase. *Language, 39,* 1–13. [12]

Brazelton, T. B., Koslowski, B. & Main, M. (1974). The origins of reciprocity: the early mother–infant interaction. In M. Lewis & L. A. Rosenblum (Eds.) *The effect of the infant on its care-giver.* New York: Wiley. [57, 62]

Brown, R. (1958). How shall a thing be called? *Psychological Review, 65,* 14–21. [45]

Brown, R. (1968). The development of Wh questions in child speech. *Journal of Verbal Learning and Verbal Behavior, 7,* 279–90. [67]

Brown, R. (1973). *A first language.* Cambridge, Mass.: Harvard University Press. [1, 14, 67, 137]

Brown, R. & Fraser, C. (1963). The acquisition of syntax. In C. Cofer & B. Musgrave (Eds.) *Verbal behavior and learning: problems and processes.* New York: McGraw-Hill. [12]

Brown, R. & Gilman, A. (1960). The pronouns of power and solidarity. In T. A. Sebeok (Ed.) *Style in language.* Cambridge, Mass.: M.I.T. Press. [59]

Bruner, J. (1975a). From communication to language. *Cognition, 3,* 255–87. [8, 24, 29, 40–1, 45, 48, 114]

Bruner, J. (1975b). The ontogenesis of speech acts. *Journal of Child Language, 2,* 1–19. [24, 29, 41, 45–6]

Bruner, J. & Sherwood, V. (1976). Peekaboo and the learning of rule structure. In J. Bruner, A. Jolly & K. Sylva (Eds.) *Play.* Harmondsworth, Middx.: Penguin. [63]

Buhler, K. (1934). *Sprachtheorie: die Darstellungsfunktion der Sprache.* Jena: Fischer. [24]

Campbell, R. & Wales, R. (1970). The study of language acquisition. In J. Lyons (Ed.) *New horizons in linguistics.* Harmondsworth, Middx.: Penguin. [24, 57]

Cassirer, E. (1923). *The philosophy of symbolic forms,* Vol. 1: *Language.* Trans. by R. Manheim. New Haven: Yale University Press, 1953. [24]

Chafe, W. (1970). *Meaning and the structure of language.* Chicago: University of Chicago Press. [16]

Chomsky, N. (1957). *Syntactic structures.* The Hague: Mouton. [11, 13]

Chomsky, N. (1959). Review of *Verbal behavior* by B. F. Skinner. *Language, 35,* 26–58. [12]

Chomsky, N. (1965). *Aspects of the theory of syntax.* Cambridge, Mass.: M.I.T. Press. [13, 15]

Cicourel, A. V. (1972). Basic and normative rules in the negotiation of status and role. In D. Sudnow (Ed.) *Studies in social interaction.* New York: The Free Press. [59]

Clark, E. (1973). What's in a word? On the child's acquisition of semantics in his first language. In T. E. Moore (Ed.) *Cognitive development and the acquisition of language.* New York: Academic Press. [38–40, 41, 112, 115–6]

Collis, G. M. (1977). Visual co-orientation and maternal speech. In H. R. Schaffer (Ed.) *Studies in mother–infant interaction.* London: Academic Press. [46, 47]

Collis, G. M. & Schaffer, H. R. (1975). Synchronization of visual attention in mother–infant pairs. *Journal of Child Psychology and Psychiatry, 16,* 315–20. [46, 47]

Corrigan, R. (1978). Language development as related to Stage 6 object permanence development. *Journal of Child Language, 5,* 173–89. [20, 21]

Cruse, D. (1977). A note on the learning of colour names. *Journal of Child Language, 4,* 305–11. [112]

De Long, A. J. (1974). Kinesic signals at utterance boundaries in preschool children. *Semiotica, 11,* 43–73. [67, 69]

Dewey, J. (1894). The psychology of infant language. *Psychological Review, 1,* 63–6. [23]

Dittmann, A. T. (1972). Developmental factors in conversational behavior. *Journal of Communication, 22,* 404–23. [67]

Dittmann, A. T. & Llewellyn, L. G. (1968). Relationship between vocalizations and head nods as listener responses. *Journal of Personality and Social Psychology, 9,* 79–84. [60]

Dore, J. (1973). The development of speech acts. Unpublished doctoral dissertation. City University of New York. [24, 26, 36, 79, 84–5]

Dore, J. (1975). Holophrases, speech acts and language and universals. *Journal of Child Language, 2,* 21–40. [15, 16, 27, 79, 84–5]

Dore, J. (1978). Conditions for the acquisition of speech acts. In I. Markova (Ed.) *The social context of language.* New York: Wiley. [26–7, 30–1]

Dore, J. (1979). What's so conceptual about the acquisition of linguistic structures? *Journal of Child Language, 6,* 129–37. [19]

Duncan, S. (1972). Some signals and rules for taking speaking turns in conversations. *Journal of Personality and Social Psychology, 3,* 283–92. [58, 60, 61]

Duncan, S. & Fiske, D. W. (1977). *Face-to-face interaction: research, methods, and theory.* Hillsdale, N.J.: Erlbaum. [58]

Edwards, D. (1973). Sensory-motor intelligence and semantic relations in early child grammar. *Cognition, 2,* 395–434. [14, 111]

Ekman, P. & Friesen, W. V. (1969). The repertoire of nonverbal behavior. *Semiotica, 1,* 49–98. [58]

Ervin-Tripp, S. & Miller, W. (1977). Early discourse, some questions about questions. In M. Lewis & L. A. Rosenblum (Eds.) *Interaction, conversation, and the development of language.* New York: Wiley. [67]

Fillmore, C. (1968). The case for case. In E. Bach & R. Harms (Eds.) *Universals in linguistic theory.* New York: Holt, Rinehart & Winston. [13, 16–17, 41, 82]

Fodor, J. & Garrett, M. (1966). Some reflections on competence and performance. In J. Lyons & R. Wales (Eds.) *Psycholinguistics Papers.* Edinburgh University Press. [12]

Fogel, A. (1977). Temporal organization in mother–infant face-to-face interaction. In H. R. Schaffer (Ed.) *Studies in mother–infant interaction.* London: Academic Press. [57, 62, 63]

Freedle, R. & Lewis, M. (1977). Prelinguistic conversations. In M. Lewis & L. A. Rosenblum (Eds.) *Interaction, conversation, and the development of language.* New York: Wiley. [57]

Furth, H. (1969). *Piaget and knowledge.* Englewood Cliffs, N.J.: Prentice–Hall. [52]

Garfinkel, H. (1972). Studies of the routine grounds of everyday activities. In D. Sudnow (Ed.) *Studies in social interaction.* New York: The Free Press. [59]

Garnica, O. K. (1977). Some prosodic and paralinguistic features of speech to young children. In C. Snow & C. A. Ferguson (Eds.) *Talking to children: language input and acquisition.* Cambridge: Cambridge University Press. [129]

Garvey, C. & Hogan, R. (1973). Social speech and social interaction: egocentrism revisited. *Child Development, 44,* 562–8. [69]

Gleason, J. B. (1973). Code switching in children's language. In T. E. Moore (Ed.) *Cognitive development and the acquisition of language.* New York: Academic Press. [69]

Glucksberg, S., Krauss, R. & Higgins, T. (1975). The development of referential communication skills. In F. Horowitz (Ed.) *Review of child development research* (Vol. 4). Chicago: University of Chicago Press. [57, 68]

Goldin-Meadow, S., Seligman, M. & Gelman, R. (1976). Language in the two-year old. *Cognition, 4,* 189–202. [113]

Gratch, G. (1975). Recent studies based on Piaget's view of object concept development. In L. Cohen & P. Salapatek (Eds.) *Infant perception* (Vol. 2). New York: Academic Press. [42]

Greenfield, P. & Smith, J. (1976). *The structure of communication in early language development.* New York: Academic Press. [16, 17–19, 21, 36, 37, 41, 68, 79, 80–4, 114]

Grice, H. P. (1957). Meaning. *Philosophical Review, 68,* 377–88. [3–6, 149]

Grice, H. P. (1968). Utterer's meaning, sentence meaning, and word-meaning. *Foundations of Language, 4,* 1–18. [4n, 7]

Grice, H. P. (1975). Logic and conversation. In P. Cole & J. L. Morgan (Eds.) *Syntax and semantics,* Vol. 3: *Speech acts.* New York: Academic Press. [58]

Grice, H. P. (1978). Further notes on logic and conversation. In P. Cole (Ed.) *Syntax and semantics,* Vol. 9: *Pragmatics.* New York: Academic Press. [58]

Habermas, J. (1970). Introductory remarks to a theory of communicative competence. In H. P. Dreitzel (Ed.) *Recent sociology* (no. 2). London: Macmillan. [24]

Halliday, M. A. K. (1975). *Learning how to mean.* London: Edward Arnold. [24, 31–6, 41, 44, 50, 51, 67, 72, 74, 79–80, 102, 116]

Harris, P. L. (1975). Development of search and object permanence during infancy. *Psychological Bulletin, 82,* 332–44. [42]

Harrison, B. (1972). *Meaning and structure.* London: Harper & Row. [38, 45, 112]

Hockett, C. (1958). *A course in modern linguistics.* New York: Macmillan. [11]

Hook, S. (Ed.) (1969). *Language and philosophy.* New York: New York University Press. [12]

Hymes, D. (1971). Competence and performance in linguistic theory. In R. Huxley & E. Ingram (Eds.) *Language acquisition: models and methods.* London: Academic Press. [57]

Ingram, D. (1971). Transitivity in child language. *Language, 47,* 888–910. [41]

Ingram, D. (1974). Stages in the development of one-word utterances. Paper presented to Stanford Child Language Forum, April 1974. [40, 41]

Jaffe, J., Stern, D. N. & Peery, J. C. (1973). "Conversational" coupling of gaze behavior in prelinguistic human development. *Journal of Psycholinguistic Research, 2,* 321–9. [57]

Katz, J. J. (1977). *Propositional structure and illocutionary force.* New York: Thomas Y. Crowell. [101n]

Kaye, K. (1977). Toward the origin of dialogue. In H. R. Schaffer (Ed.) *Studies in mother–infant interaction.* London: Academic Press. [57, 61, 62, 63]

Keenan, E. O. (1974). Conversational competence in children. *Journal of Child Language, 1,* 163–83. [69]

Keenan, E. O. & Schieffelin, B. B. (1976). Topic as a discourse notion: a study of topic in the conversations of children and adults. In C. Li (Ed.) *Subject and topic.* New York: Academic Press. [67]

Kendon, A. (1967). Some functions of gaze-direction in social interaction. *Acta Psychologica, 26,* 22–47. [61, 64]

Kendon, A. (1978). Looking in conversation and the regulation of turns at talk. *British Journal of Social and Clinical Psychology, 17,* 23–4. [64]

Kohler, W. (1925). *The mentality of apes.* Trans. by E. Winter. London: Kegan Paul, 1925. [49]

Kozhevnikov, V. & Chistovich, L. (1965). *Speech, articulation, and perception.* Washington, D.C.: U.S. Department of Commerce, Joint Publication Research Service. [54]

Labov, W. & Labov, T. (1978). Learning the syntax of questions. In R. Campbell & P. Smith (Eds.) *Recent advances in the psychology of language* (4b). London: Plenum Press. [67]

Lakoff, G. (1971). On generative semantics. In D. Steinberg & L. Jakobovitz (Eds.) *Semantics: an interdisciplinary reader in philosophy, linguistics, and psychology.* Cambridge: Cambridge University Press. [13]

Leopold, W. (1939–49). *Speech development of a bilingual child.* Vol. 1: *Vocabulary growth in the first two years.* Vol. 2: *Sound learning in the first two years.* Vol. 3: *Grammar and general problems in the first two years.* Vol. 4: *Diary from age two.* Evanston, Ill.: Northwestern University Press. [41, 50, 51, 67]

Lewis, D. K. (1969). *Convention.* Cambridge, Mass.: Harvard University Press. [7]

Lewis, M. M. (1936). *Infant speech.* London: Routledge & Kegan Paul. [67, 72, 129]

Lewis, M. & Freedle, R. (1973). Mother–infant dyad: the cradle of meaning. In P. Pliner, L. Krames & T. Alloway (Eds.) *Communication and affect.* New York: Academic Press. [57]

Lieven, E. (1979). Conversations between mothers and young children: individual differences and their implications for the study of language learning. In N. Waterson and C. Snow (Eds.) *The development of communication.* London: Wiley. [67]

Lieven, E. (1978b). Turn-taking and pragmatics: two issues in early child language. In R. Campbell & P. Smith (Eds.) *Recent advances in the psychology of language* (4a). London: Plenum Press. [67]

Lieven, E. & McShane, J. (1978). Language is a developing social skill. In D. Chivers & J. Herbert (Eds.) *Recent advances in primatology* (Vol. 1). London: Academic Press. [26]

Lyons, J. (1967). A note on possessive, existential, and locative sentences. *Foundations of Language, 3,* 390–6. [75n]

McCawley, J. (1968). The role of semantics in a grammar. In E. Bach & R. Harms (Eds.) *Universals in linguistic theory.* New York: Holt, Rinehart & Winston. [13]

Macnamara, J. (1977). From sign to language. In J. Macnamara (Ed.) *Language learning and thought.* New York: Academic Press. [129]

McNeill, D. (1966). Developmental psycholinguistics. In F. Smith & G. Miller (Eds.) *The genesis of language.* Cambridge, Mass.: M.I.T. Press. [12]

McNeill, D. (1970). *The acquisition of language.* New York: Harper & Row. [15, 19, 40, 114]

McNeill, D. (1975). Semiotic extension. In R. L. Solso (Ed.) *Information processing and cognition: the Loyola symposium.* Hillsdale, N.J.: Erlbaum. [54, 101n]

Malinowski, B. (1923). The problem of meaning in primitive languages.

Appendix to C. K. Ogden & I. A. Richards, *The meaning of meaning.* London: Routledge & Kegan Paul. [129]

Menyuk, P. (1963). Syntactic features in the language of children. *Child Development, 34*, 407–22. [12]

Menyuk, P. & Bernholtz, N. (1969). Prosodic features and children's language development. *Quarterly Progress Reports of the Research Laboratory of Electronics* (M.I.T.), *93*, 216–9. [29]

Miller, W. & Ervin, S. (1964). The development of grammar in child language. In U. Bellugi & R. Brown (Eds.) *Monographs of the Society for Research in Child Development, 29*, (1, serial no. 92). [12]

Morehead, D. & Morehead, A. (1974). From signal to sign. In R. Schiefelbusch & L. Lloyd (Eds.) *Language perspectives – acquisition, retardation, and intervention.* London: Macmillan. [54]

Murphy, C. M. (1978). Pointing in the context of a shared activity. *Child Development, 49*, 371–80. [47–8]

Murphy, C. M. & Messer, D. J. (1977). Mothers, infants, and pointing: a study of gesture. In H. R. Schaffer (Ed.) *Studies in mother–infant interaction.* London: Academic Press. [46–7]

Neisser, U. (1967). *Cognitive psychology.* New York: Appleton-Century-Crofts. [45]

Nelson, K. (1973). Structure and strategy in learning to talk. *Monographs of the Society for Research in Child Development, 38* (1–2, serial no. 149). [1, 19, 22–3, 36, 37, 42, 44, 50, 51]

Nelson, K. (1974). Concept, word, and sentence. *Psychological Review, 81*, 267–85. [35, 39, 42–4, 55]

Nelson, K. (1975). The nominal shift in semantic–syntactic development. *Cognitive Psychology, 7*, 461–79. [37]

Newson, J. & Newson, E. (1975). Intersubjectivity and the transmission of culture: on the social origins of symbolic functioning. *Bulletin of the British Psychological Society, 28*, 437–46. [54]

Ninio, A. & Bruner, J. (1978). The achievement and antecedents of labelling. *Journal of Child Language, 5*, 1–15. [8, 47–8, 49, 146]

Olson, D. (1970). Language and thought: aspects of a cognitive theory of semantics. *Psychological Review, 77*, 257–73. [29, 45, 48]

Parisi, D. & Antinucci, F. (1973). *Essentials of grammar.* Trans. by E. Bates. New York: Academic Press, 1976. [29]

Piaget, J. (1923). *The language and thought of the child.* Trans. by M. Gabain. London: Routledge & Kegan Paul, 1926. [68]

Piaget, J. (1937). *The construction of reality in the child.* Trans. by M. Cook. London: Routledge & Kegan Paul, 1955. [14, 41]

Piaget, J. (1945). *Play, dreams and imitation in childhood.* Trans. by C. Gattegno & F. M. Hodgson. London: Routledge & Kegan Paul, 1951. [35, 51–4, 55]

Piaget, J. & Inhelder, B. (1966). *The psychology of the child.* Trans. by H. Weaver. New York: Basic Books, 1969. [52]

Quine, W. V. O. (1960). *Word and object.* Cambridge, Mass.: M.I.T. Press. [38]

Remick, H. (1976). Maternal speech to children during language acquisition. In W. von Raffler-Engel & Y. Lebrun (Eds.) *Baby talk and infant speech.* Lisse: Swets & Zeitlinger. [68]

Rheingold, H. L., Gewirtz, J. L. & Ross, H. W. (1959). Conditioning of vocalizations in infants. *Journal of Comparative and Physiological Psychology, 52,* 68–73. [66]

Richards, M. P. M. (1974). First steps in becoming social. In M. P. M. Richards (Ed.) *The integration of a child into a social world.* Cambridge: Cambridge University Press. [8]

Ricks, D. (1971). The beginnings of vocal communication in infants and autistic children. Unpublished M.D. thesis. University of London. [30]

Ricks, D. (1975). Vocal communication in pre-verbal normal and autistic children. In N. O'Connor (Ed.) *Language, cognitive deficits, and retardation.* London: Butterworth. [30]

Rommetveit, R. (1974). *On message structure.* New York: Wiley. [29, 45, 59]

Rosch, E., Mervis, C., Gray, W., Johnston, D. & Boyes-Braem, P. (1976). Basic objects in natural categories. *Cognitive Psychology, 8,* 382–439. [39]

Ross, J. (1970). On declarative sentences. In R. Jacobs & P. Rosenbaum (Eds.) *Readings in English transformational grammar.* Waltham, Mass.: Ginn. [13]

Rutter, D. R., Stephenson, G. M., Ayling, K. & White, P. A. (1978). The timing of looks in dyadic conversation. *British Journal of Social and Clinical Psychology, 17,* 17–21. [61, 64]

Ryan, J. (1974). Early language development. In M. P. M. Richards (Ed.) *The integration of a child into a social world.* Cambridge: Cambridge University Press. [8–9, 24]

Sachs, J., Brown, R. & Salerno, R. (1976). Adults' speech to children. In W. von Raffler-Engel & Y. Lebrun (Eds.) *Baby talk and infant speech.* Lisse: Swets & Zeitlinger. [68]

Sacks, H., Schegloff, E. & Jefferson, G. (1974). A simplest systematics for the organization of turn-taking for conversation. *Language, 50,* 696–735. [58, 59, 60, 94, 126]

Sadock, J. M. (1978). On testing for conversational implicature. In P. Cole (Ed.) *Syntax and semantics,* vol. 9: *Pragmatics.* New York: Academic Press. [58]

Sassure, F. de (1916). *Course in general linguistics.* Trans. by W. Baskin. New York: Philosophical Library, 1955. [24]

Scaife, M. & Bruner, J. (1975). The capacity for joint visual attention in the infant. *Nature, 253,* 265–6. [46]

Schafer, P. (1922). Beobachtungen und versuche an einem kind. *Zeitschrift pädegogische Psychologie, 23,* 269–89. [129]

Schaffer, H. R., Collis, G. M. & Parsons, G. (1977). Vocal interchange and visual regard in verbal and pre-verbal children. In H. R. Schaffer (Ed.) *Studies in mother–infant interaction.* London: Academic Press. [63]

Schegloff, E. (1968). Sequencing in conversational openings. *American Anthropologist, 70,* 1075–95. [58, 59]

Schegloff, E. & Sacks, H. (1973). Opening up closings. *Semiotica, 8,* 289–327. [58]

Schiffer, S. (1972). *Meaning.* Oxford: Oxford University Press. [4, 7, 149, 150]

Schlesinger, I. (1971). Production of utterances and language acquisition. In D. I. Slobin (Ed.) *The ontogenesis of grammar.* New York: Academic Press. [12, 13]

Searle, J. (1969). *Speech acts.* Cambridge: Cambridge University Press. [4–5n, 5, 24, 25]

Shatz, M. (1978). On the development of communicative understandings. *Cognitive Psychology, 10,* 271–301. [25]

Shatz, M. & Gelman, R. (1973). The development of communication skills: modifications in the speech of young children as a function of the listener. *Monographs of the Society for Research in Child Development, 38,* (5, serial no. 152). [69]

Sinclair, H. (1970). The transition from sensory-motor behaviour to symbolic activity. *Interchange, 1,* 119–26. [54]

Sinclair, H. (1971). Sensorimotor action patterns as a condition for the acquisition of syntax. In R. Huxley & E. Ingram (Eds.) *Language acquisition: models and methods.* London: Academic Press. [54]

Sinclair, H. (1973). Language acquisition and cognitive development. In T. E. Moore (Eds.) *Cognitive development and the acquisition of language.* New York: Academic Press. [54]

Skinner, B. (1957). *Verbal behavior.* New York: Appleton-Century-Crofts. [12]

Smith, M. (1933). The influence of age, sex, and situation on the frequency, form, and function of questions asked by preschool children. *Child Development, 4,* 201–13. [67, 137]

Snow, C. (1972). Mothers' speech to children learning language. *Child Development, 43,* 549–65. [68]

Snow, C. (1977a). The development of conversation between mothers and babies. *Journal of Child Language, 4,* 1–22. [8, 48, 57, 66, 68, 126]

Snow, C. (1977b). Mothers' speech research: from input to interaction. In C. Snow & C. A. Ferguson (Eds.) *Talking to children: language input and acquisition.* Cambridge: Cambridge University Press. [69, 126]

Stampe, D. W. (1975). Meaning and truth in the theory of speech acts. In P. Cole & J. L. Morgan (Eds.) *Syntax and semantics,* Vol. 3: *Speech acts.* New York: Academic Press. [5–6]

Stern, D. N. (1974). Mother and infant at play: the dyadic interaction involving facial, vocal, and gaze behaviors. In M. Lewis & L. A. Rosenblum (Eds.) *The effect of the infant on its caregiver*. New York: Wiley. [57, 62, 63]

Stern, D. N., Beebe, B., Jaffe, J. & Bennett, S. L. (1977). The infant's stimulus world during social interaction: a study of caregiver behaviours with particular reference to repetition and timing. In H. R. Schaffer (Ed.) *Studies in mother–infant interaction*. London: Academic Press. [57, 62]

Stevenson, A. (1893). The speech of children. *Science*, *21*, 118–20. [40]

Sugarman-Bell, S. (1978). Some organizational aspects of pre-verbal communication. In I. Markova (Ed.) *The social context of language*. New York: Wiley. [28, 118–9, 145]

Todd, G. A. & Palmer, B. (1968). Social reinforcement of infant babbling. *Child Development*, *39*, 591–6. [66]

Tonkova-Yampol'skaya, R. V. (1969). Development of speech intonation in infants during the first two years of life. *Soviet Psychology*, *7*, 48–54. [29]

Trevarthen, C. (1977). Descriptive analyses of infant communicative behaviour. In H. R. Schaffer (Ed.) *Studies in mother–infant interaction*. London: Academic Press. [57, 65–6]

Tyack, D. & Ingram, D. (1977). Children's production and comprehension of questions. *Journal of Child Language*, *4*, 211–24. [67, 137]

Vorster, J. (1975). Mommy linguist: the case for motherese. *Lingua*, *37*, 281–312. [69, 126]

Vygotsky, L. (1934). *Thought and language*. Trans. by E. Hanfman & G. Vakar. Cambridge, Mass.: M.I.T. Press, 1962. [50]

Walker, R. (1975). Conversational implicatures. In S. Blackburn (Ed.) *Meaning, reference and necessity*. Cambridge: Cambridge University Press. [58]

Weisberg, P. (1963). Social and nonsocial conditioning of infant vocalizations. *Child Development*, *34*, 377–88. [66]

Werner, H. & Kaplan, B. (1963). *Symbol formation*. New York: Wiley. [29, 35, 50]

Wilson, N. L. (1970). Grice on meaning: the ultimate counterexample. *Nous*, *4*, 295–304. [4–5n]

Wittgenstein, L. (1953). *Philosophical investigations*. Oxford: Blackwell. [38]

Wolff, P. H. (1969). The natural history of crying and other vocalizations in early infancy. In B. M. Foss (Ed.) *Determinants of infant behaviour* (vol. 4). London: Methuen. [8]

Yngve, V. H. (1970). On getting a word in edgewise. *Papers from the sixth regional meeting of the Chicago Linguistic Society*. Chicago: Chicago Linguistic Society. [60]

Ziff, P. (1967). On H. P. Grice's account of meaning. *Analysis*, *28*, 1–8. [4–5n, 151]

Subject index